No Longe
EWU

NATURAL MONOPOLY

AND ITS

REGULATION

No Longer Property of
EWU Libraries

NATURAL MONOPOLY

AND ITS

REGULATION

30TH ANNIVERSARY EDITION
WITH A NEW PREFACE BY THE AUTHOR

RICHARD A. POSNER

CATO INSTITUTE

WASHINGTON, D.C.

CALS
HD2757.2
.P67
1999

Copyright 1999 by the Cato Institute.
All rights reserved.

Library of Congress Cataloging-in-Publication Data

Posner, Richard A.
    Natural monopoly and its regulation / Richard A. Posner.
      p. cm.
    "30th anniversary edition with a new preface by the author."
    Includes bibliographical references.
    ISBN 1-882577-81-7
    1. Monopolies.   2. Monopolies—Government policy.   3. Trade
regulation.   4. Antitrust law.   I. Title.
HD2757.2.P67   1999
338.8'2—DC21   99-22490
                                                  CIP

Printed in the United States of America.

CATO INSTITUTE
1000 Massachusetts Ave., N.W.
Washington, D.C. 20001

EASTERN WASHINGTON
UNIVERSITY LIBRARIES
CHENEY, WA 99004

Preface

It is a curious experience to reread an article that one wrote thirty years ago. Not that this is the first time I have reread "Natural Monopoly and Its Regulation." I am sure I reread it from time to time in the five years or so after it was published, when I was writing extensively on regulated industries. But it has probably been at least a quarter of a century since I looked at the article.

What struck me most forcibly in rereading it while composing this foreword to the republished article is how tame it now seems. I imagine that most lawyers and economists reading it today would find nothing very startling in it, whether or not they accepted its bold thesis that public utility and common carrier regulation[1] are more trouble than they are worth even in the diminishing number of industries that have pronounced natural-monopoly characteristics, that is, in which average costs decline over so large a range of outputs that a single firm would have a big cost advantage over multiple firms serving the same market.

But in 1969 not only the thesis but also much of the analysis was distinctly heterodox. Not that there wasn't even then a large literature in economics and in law that was critical of the operation of public utility and common carrier regulation. But the focus of this literature was on ways of improving the operation of the regulatory process to make it a more effective constraint on monopoly pricing, predatory pricing, and other supposed dangers of unregulated monopoly. It was not on deregulation, a term rarely used back then and a concept that was not on the policy agenda. The emphasis on reforming rather than abolishing regulation reflected the fact that most economists and lawyers had considerable faith in government—and considerable

---

[1]These are essentially synonymous. The term "public utility" tends to be used in power industries and the term "common carrier" in transportation and communications. Somewhat similar controls are (diminishingly) found in financial services industries, primarily banking, but under different names.

distrust of free markets. To put this differently, they had far more sensitive antennas for sources of "market failure" than for sources of "government failure." The former were thought systemic, the latter the product of accident, such as poor appointments to regulatory agencies or corrigible errors in the means of regulation. It was more or less assumed that if a source of market failure (such as declining average costs over the feasible range of output) could be identified, a scheme of regulation could readily be devised and administered that would yield a net increment in social welfare. The benefit-cost ratio of regulation was, in other words, assumed to exceed one.

This assumption was questioned mainly at the University of Chicago, by economists like Milton Friedman, George Stigler, Aaron Director, Harold Demsetz, and Ronald Coase, and by a few lawyers, such as Edmund Kitch. Although I was not yet teaching at Chicago when I wrote and published my article, I was already familiar with the "Chicago School," in part through reading and in part through having gotten to know one of its illustrious members, Aaron Director; he had retired to California and had an office in the Stanford Law School, where I was teaching. I had also developed a certain skepticism about regulation from my work on the staff of President Johnson's Task Force on Telecommunications Policy during the year (1967–68) before I began teaching at Stanford. I had seen the regulation of the telecommunications industry at close quarters and been unimpressed. This experience, rather than any conservative or libertarian ideology—for until I began teaching, I considered myself a liberal Democrat—made me receptive to the Chicago School's critique of regulation.

"Natural Monopoly and Its Regulation" was the first article I had ever written, and it is synoptic rather than original. Or if it is original, it is so in drawing together a scattered literature and extracting from it the implication that had rarely been made express, that we would be better off without trying to regulate natural monopolies. I did not deny that unregulated natural monopoly would yield various inefficiencies, primarily the reduction in output that comes about when a monopolist charges a price in excess of cost.[2] But I thought them ex-

---

[2]Notice that I do not say *marginal* cost. In a situation of declining average cost, setting price equal to marginal cost will produce bankruptcy. The efficient pricing system in such a situation is called "Ramsey pricing" and involves systematic departures from marginal cost. But the overall price level will be lower, and output higher, than under a system of unregulated monopoly pricing. See Richard A. Posner, *Economic Analysis of Law* 389–390 (5th ed. 1998).

aggerated, and the noneconomic objections shallow. One of the noneconomic points I made, which on rereading my article strikes me as still somewhat fresh, is that a natural monopolist who exploits his monopoly position to obtain large profits is ethically no different from the owner of a scarce natural resource who earns large economic rents by virtue of its scarcity; the natural monopolist's "market power [and resulting profits] flows from the cost and demand characteristics of the market in which he is selling, rather than from unfair or restrictive tactics or from legal privileges."[3]

The article particularly emphasizes the practical difficulties of constraining a monopolist's pricing. The effort to constrain, I argue, is more likely to produce distortions than to bring about a reasonable simulacrum of competitive pricing and output. This is primarily because of information and incentive problems of regulators and because of efforts by the regulated firms to neutralize regulation or to bend it to their advantage. These sources of "regulatory failure," which is likely to be more serious than the "market failure" that regulation is supposed to correct, are now widely recognized. A position that in 1969 was decidedly outside the mainstream of economic and legal thinking about regulated industries is now thoroughly orthodox. This is not to say, even today, that most economists want to deregulate the local telephone and electrical companies, which are the principal remaining natural monopolists; there is still a case to be made for the regulation of natural monopoly, though one I still find unconvincing. Which is to say only that what was thirty years ago a tendency to facilely invoke "market failure" as a more or less automatic justification for public utility or common carrier regulation is today a wary skepticism, a demand for proof. To the extent that my article raised doubts about public utility and common carrier regulation even where the utility or carrier was a genuine natural monopolist, it a fortiori undermined the case for such regulation of firms that were not natural monopolists, such as producers of natural gas, trucking companies, and airlines.

I do not, of course, take credit for the deregulation movement, which has greatly reduced the scope of public utility and common carrier regulation, and, I am happy to say, with generally very good

[3]This volume, p. 19.

results.[4] The causality is complex,[5] and academic advocacy probably played only a very small role.[6] What mainly happened is that regulation broke down; it was a microcosm of the breakdown of the Soviet Union's command-and-control economy. This is not the place to explore that history. A combination of inflation in the 1970s and accelerating technological change favorable to competition (the latter a challenge to regulation that was already visible in 1969[7]) brought about a situation in which regulation no longer satisfied the needs of key interest groups, whether of regulated firms or of customers. It is not inevitable that technological change should weaken rather than strengthen the forces of monopoly and resulting demand for regulation. If the change took the form of increasing economies of scale, as well it might, it would make natural monopoly more rather than less common and so strengthen the case for regulation. But the change has been in the opposite direction. Natural monopolies have crumbled; even the local natural monopolies, which are based on the inefficiency of duplicating a local grid of wires or pipes, may soon go the way of the former natural monopoly of long-distance telephone service. When there are no more natural monopolies, my article will indeed be merely a historical curiosity.

[4]See Richard A. Posner, "The Effects of Deregulation on Competition: The Experience of the United States" (forthcoming in *Fordham International Law Journal*), and references cited there.

[5]See Joseph D. Kearney and Thomas W. Merrill, "The Great Transformation of Regulated Industries Law," 98 *Columbia Law Review* 1323, 1383–1403 (1998).

[6]Kearney and Merrill assign it a larger role than I would be inclined to do. See id. at 1397–1403.

[7]This volume, p. 106.

Natural Monopoly and Its Regulation

A firm that is the only seller of a product or service having no close substitutes is said to enjoy a monopoly.[1] Monopoly is an important concept to this Article but even more important is the related but somewhat less familiar concept of "natural monopoly." The term does not refer to the actual number of sellers in a market but to the relationship between demand and the technology of supply. If the entire demand within a relevant market can be satisfied at lowest cost by one firm rather than by two or more, the market is a natural monopoly, whatever the actual number of firms in it. If such a market contains more than one firm, either the firms will quickly shake down to one through mergers or failures, or production will continue to consume more resources than necessary. In the first case competition is short-lived and in the second it produces inefficient results. Competition is thus not a viable regulatory mechanism under conditions of natural monopoly. Hence, it is said, direct controls are necessary to ensure satisfactory performance: controls over profits, specific rates, quality of service, extensions and abandonments of service and plant, even permission whether to enter the business at all. This set of controls has been applied mainly to gas, water, and electric power companies, where it is known as "public utility regulation," and to providers of public transportation and telecommunications, where it is known as "common carrier regulation." (I shall

I wish to thank all who read and criticized earlier drafts of this Article; and to acknowledge a special debt to four with whom discussion of the issues examined herein has greatly clarified and enlarged my own thinking—William F. Baxter, Aaron Director, Leland L. Johnson, and Leonard M. Ross.
[1]Throughout this Article, the terms "monopoly" and "monopolistic" will be used to refer to single-firm monopoly, rather than in the more familiar current sense in which any market that is not perfectly competitive may be said to have monopolistic elements. One should note that the market need not be nationwide. A product or service can be effectively monopolized although provided by different firms in different areas of the country, if buyers in one area are prevented by transportation or other barriers from shopping among the firms.

1

use "regulation" or "public utility regulation" to refer to both.) The question that this Article addresses is whether natural monopoly provides an adequate justification for the imposition of these regulatory controls.[2]

A critical examination of this question seems timely. The terms "public utility" and "common carrier" may have rather an antique ring, but they also have important contemporary applications. The regulated industries provide the essential infrastructure of modern industrial society. They are also on the frontiers of technological progress. The principal civilian use of nuclear energy has been electrical generation, the principal commercial application of space technology satellite communications; both are regulated services. We are also witnessing the emergence of immensely promising industries, such as cable television, that may have sufficient natural monopoly characteristics to invite extension of the regulatory principle to them. And it is even intimated that the extension of price controls to the economy at large must be seriously considered.[3]

As a perusal of the citations in this Article will disclose, the 1960's have seen an upsurge of scholarly interest in the regulatory field

----

[2]The reader may question whether natural monopoly has much to do with regulation of the transportation industries. Even in the case of the railroads, the initial regulatory thrust, at least at the federal level, was to reduce competition among the regulated firms; proponents of regulation charged that there was too much competition rather than too little. See Hilton, *The Consistency of the Interstate Commerce Act,* 9 J. LAW & ECON, 87 (1966). See generally G. KOLKO, RAILROADS AND REGULATION 1877–1916 (1965). This theme is even clearer in the regulation of inland-water carriers, airlines, and motor carriers. See C. FULDA, COMPETITION IN THE REGULATED INDUSTRIES: TRANSPORTATION 12, 16, 20–21 (1961); L. KEYES, FEDERAL CONTROL OF ENTRY INTO AIR TRANSPORTATION 83, 85 (1951); 71 YALE L.J. 307, 308–09 (1961). But in all of these instances, prominent among the conditions alleged to justify regulation were those conventionally associated with tendencies to natural monopoly: excess capacity, price discrimination, and "ruinous" price wars. See, e.g., *Coordination of Motor Transportation,* 182 I.C.C. 263, 362 (1932); L. KEYES, *supra* at 90–92, 103–04. In some instances, to be sure— trucking is a good example—the allegation of natural monopoly is preposterous. One reason for regulating trucking, however, was to protect a discriminatory pattern of railroad pricing that had arisen in the era when the railroad industry had pronounced natural monopoly features. See note 121 *infra* and accompanying text. Natural monopoly is thus a basic, albeit not the only, theme of transportation regulation. To the extent that public utility regulation can be justified on grounds unrelated to natural monopoly (I cannot myself think of any such ground), the critique of this Article is inapplicable.

[3]See Kaysen, *Model-Makers and Decision-Makers: Economists and the Policy Process,* THE PUBLIC INTEREST, Summer 1968, at 80, 89–90.

after many years of comparative neglect. The Brookings Institution is supporting an ambitious program of study in the field. Several high-level federal policy groups, including the President's Task Force on Communications Policy[4] and the Cabinet Committee on Price Stability, have recently addressed particular aspects of regulation. But what has been lacking thus far is an attempt to evaluate its basic soundness. Much criticized in the details of its application, regulation is assumed by nearly all who work or write in the field, as by the public in general, to be fundamentally inevitable, wise, and necessary. However, personal experience as a government lawyer involved in regulatory matters made me skeptical about the validity of the assumption and this study has convinced me that in fact public utility regulation is probably not a useful exertion of governmental powers; that its benefits cannot be shown to outweigh its costs; and that even in markets where efficiency dictates monopoly we might do better to allow natural economic forces to determine business conduct and performance subject only to the constraints of antitrust policy. I would stress, however, that no general challenge to government regulation of business is intended. One regulatory framework whose continued existence is explicitly presupposed by my analysis is, as just mentioned, the antitrust laws. Regulations enforcing standards of health or safety are instances of the many other government constraints on business activity that lie outside the scope of my critique.

The Article, in four parts, attempts to (1) identify areas of behavior (such as prices and profits) where an unregulated natural monopolist might pursue policies contrary to the welfare of society; (2) describe the regulatory process as it operates today and, in a rough way, evaluate its social benefits and costs; (3) assess the possibilities of constructive reform; (4) consider some alternatives to regulation and offer some practical suggestions.

---

[4]I served with the Task Force as its general counsel in 1967–68, which will explain the frequency with which my examples are drawn from the communications industry. At this writing, the report of the Task Force to the President has not been published, but it is summarized in 34 TELECOMMUNICATIONS REPORTS, Dec. 9, 1968, at 1. Needless to say, the opinions in this Article are my own.

I. The Grounds for Regulating Prices, Entry, or Other Business Conduct in a Natural Monopoly Market

In this opening branch of the analysis, I shall have nothing directly to say about the concepts or practice of regulation. Rather, I shall ask in what respects one might expect business performance under conditions of natural monopoly to be unsatisfactory from a social standpoint. When these elements of predictably deficient performance have been isolated, it will be possible to consider the extent to which the regulatory process is responsive to actual and serious problems.

A. *Monopoly Prices and Profits*

Under competition, the price of a good to the consumer tends to be bid down by the sellers to its cost (including in cost such profit as is required to attract capital into the industry). Consumers, as a result, obtain many goods at prices that are appreciably lower than the actual value of the goods to them. Monopoly enables the seller to capture much of the extra value that would otherwise accrue to consumers. To illustrate, let us suppose that if aspirin is sold at 1 cent per half grain (its cost) there will be 200 purchasers and that if it is sold at 10 cents there will still be 100 purchasers. The monopolist who desires to maximize his profit will sell at 10 cents—the monopoly price—where his total cost will be $1 and his revenue $10, producing a supracompetitive profit of $9. Monopoly prices are widely considered to be socially undesirable because of their alleged effects on income distribution, overall economic stability, the allocation of economic resources, and proper business incentives. The arguments in support of these grounds are briefly as follows:

The effect of charging a monopoly price is to transfer wealth from the consumers of a product to the owners of the firm selling it.[5] The consumers are deprived of much of the extra value that they would enjoy in a competitive market, where they would be able to purchase at cost; the stockholders are enriched by capturing a good part of that value in increased profits. Transfers or redistributions of wealth are unavoidable in a society that is not perfectly egalitarian. At the same

---

[5]Insofar as companies retain a considerable portion of their earnings, monopoly profits may also be said to transfer wealth from consumers to corporations. That effect will be considered when we discuss the political dimension of the monopoly problem. *See* text accompanying note 85 *infra*.

time, one could argue that it is sound social policy to reduce disparities of income and wealth so far as compatible with maintaining proper incentives. The redistribution of wealth that monopoly profits effect seems inconsistent with that goal. Consumers as a class are probably less affluent than stockholders; and a monopoly profit performs no obvious incentive function (our definition of cost included a profit sufficient to keep the firm in business).

It is further argued that insufficient demand in the private sector, a cause of recession, could be aggravated by a transfer of income from consumers to investors. The latter, being a more affluent group, are apt to save a larger proportion of their income. In periods of declining demand, moreover, a monopolist may be slower to reduce price than a competitive firm. In addition, by creating higher prices than would prevail under competition monopolization might be thought to aggravate any inflationary tendencies. And since a monopolist (as we shall soon see) uses less of the factors of production than a competitive firm, monopoly might appear to promote unemployment.

The mere act of redistributing wealth between two classes of individuals, while possibly offensive to ideals of social justice or adverse to the proper working of the business cycle, is not inconsistent with obtaining maximum benefit from the nation's economic resources. But the means by which the monopolist seeks to maximize profits may create inefficiency. Suppose that a widget costs 4 cents to produce (regardless of quantity) and that the widget monopolist can sell 10,000 at 7 cents, 12,000 at 6 cents, 13,000 at 5 cents, and 14,000 at 4 cents. Given this demand schedule, the profit-maximizing monopolist will sell at 7 cents, where his total cost is $400, his total revenue $700, and his monopoly profit $300. Whether we prefer stockholders or consumers to derive the greater benefit from the production of widgets, society as a whole is worse off when the monopoly price of 7 cents is charged rather than the competitive price of 4 cents. When 14,000 are sold at the competitive price, consumers who would have taken 10,000 widgets at 7 cents derive extra value of $300 from being able to purchase at cost. This just offsets the monopolist's loss, but there are further gains: Consumers who would have purchased an additional 2,000 at a price of 6 cents derive a value of $40 above what they paid at the competitive price; and those who would have paid 5 cents each for the additional 1,000 derive extra value aggregating $10.

The total consumers' surplus when the competitive price is charged is thus $350. This sum exceeds the monopoly profit (or producer's surplus)—$300—that the seller obtained by charging a higher price.[6]

[6]Conceivably, the $50 difference between the monopoly profit obtained and the consumers' surplus sacrificed understates the economic cost of monopoly, for an extra dollar of income may be worth less to stockholders as a group than to consumers as a group, assuming the former to be richer. *See* Lerner, *The Concept of Monopoly and the Measurement of Monopoly Power,* 1 REV. ECON. STUDIES 157, 158–59 (1934), *reprinted in* READINGS IN MICROECONOMICS 239, 240–41 (W. Breit & H. Hochman eds. 1968). We shall disregard this possibility, however, in view of its highly conjectural and uncertain character. *See* T. SCITOVSKY, WELFARE AND COMPETITION: THE ECONOMICS OF A FULLY EMPLOYED ECONOMY 60 (1951); text following note 39 *infra*.

The concept that monopoly pricing causes welfare losses, illustrated in the text by a rather stylized arithmetical example, can also be represented, and perhaps more clearly, graphically. Let *dd* be the range of prices at which various quantities of widgets will sell—in other words, the demand schedule for widgets. Under competition it is evident that the equilibrium price is p_c and output O_c; for at any higher price additional output could be sold at a remunerative price—a price that exceeded the cost of the additional output (marginal cost or *MC*)—while at any lower price cost would exceed revenue. When p_c is the price charged, consumers' surplus equal to the area Ap_cC is generated, representing the additional amount that consumers could be made to pay for widgets under a system of perfect discrimination. A monopolist, on the other hand, would be free to restrict his output to O_m and charge the higher price p_m, the point from which any further reduction in price would generate less additional revenue (marginal revenue or *MR*) than additional cost. At that price consumers' surplus is reduced to the area Ap_mD and the monopolist appropriates the area Dp_mBC as monopoly profit or producers' surplus, resulting in a net diminution in welfare of p_mp_cB. That area represents the "deadweight loss" of monopoly—the part of consumers' surplus that the monopolist cannot appropriate but that the consumers lose. One should note, however, that this model of monopoly performance is highly simplified; for a number of refinements besides those I shall discuss in the text see J. ROBINSON, THE ECONOMICS OF IMPERFECT COMPETITION 143–58 (1933).

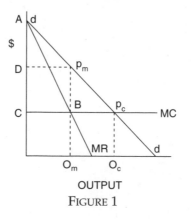

OUTPUT

FIGURE 1

The intuitive basis of the illustration is quite simple. Because the utility functions of individuals vary, the monopolist selling at a single price cannot capture the entire consumers' surplus that a sale at cost would produce. The price that captures as much as possible necessarily excludes a group of potential consumers to whom the utility of the product exceeded its cost of manufacture. The monopoly price thus prevents the economic system from meeting wants that could be met perfectly well. Consumers may be led to substitute more costly or less useful products merely because the cost of widgets to them is too high, although society's economic resources would be better used producing widgets rather than substitute products. It can also be shown that in limiting output the monopolist is underutilizing productive resources.

Finally, the ability to obtain very substantial profits without particular exertion, merely as a consequence of enjoying a monopoly, may be thought to dull incentives to efficient and progressive operation. A firm that is continuously and effortlessly very profitable may not feel much sense of urgency about reducing costs in order to obtain still greater profits.

The case for condemning monopoly prices and profits just outlined is less compelling than it perhaps first appears. It is not clear that an unregulated monopolist will normally charge a price that greatly exceeds what a nonmonopolist would charge for the same service; nor is it clear that society should be deeply concerned if a natural monopolist does charge an excessive price.

One possible ground for doubting that grossly excessive prices and profits are likely to flow from the possession of a monopoly can be derived from the theory that the large modern corporation does not seek to maximize profit.[7] The revisionist theory, as one might apply it to a monopolist, may be summarized briefly as follows: Manage-

[7]For a forceful recent exposition of the theory see J. GALBRAITH, THE NEW INDUSTRIAL STATE *passim* (1967). D. LAMBERTON, THE THEORY OF PROFIT (1965); J. MCGUIRE, THEORIES OF BUSINESS BEHAVIOR (1964); O. WILLIAMSON, THE ECONOMICS OF DISCRETIONARY BEHAVIOR: MANAGERIAL OBJECTIVES IN A THEORY OF THE FIRM 12–25 (1964); Alchian, *The Basis of Some Recent Advances in the Theory of Management of the Firm*, 14 J. IND. ECON. 30 (1965); and Machlup, *Theories of the Firm: Marginalist, Behavioral, Managerial*, 57 AM. ECON. REV. 1 (1967), contain excellent summaries of the earlier literature. For a lively debate on the question see Peterson, *Corporate Control and Capitalism*, 79 Q.J. ECON. 1 (1965); Kaysen, *Another View of Corporate Capitalism*, 79 Q.J. ECON. 41 (1965); Peterson, *Corporate Control and Capitalism: Reply*, 79 Q.J. ECON. 492 (1965). My statement of the "non-profit-maximization" or "managerial discretion" theory is perhaps overstrong. For a more cautious and hypothetical statement and analysis see O. WILLIAMSON, *supra, passim.*

ment in the large modern corporation is largely autonomous and self-perpetuating. The nominal owners, the stockholders, will assert control only if the corporation fails to produce a respectable profit, comparable to that of similar firms but not necessarily the maximum that management could extract. To be sure, if competition is sufficiently vigorous, the managers will be constrained, not by stockholders but by the market, to sell as dearly as they can while minimizing cost. Under competition, there is in theory only one profit—the return necessary to attract and hold capital—not a range of possible profits that includes a comfortable but moderate return near the bottom of that range. But it is possible that in many industries price competition is not very effective due to fewness of sellers, barriers to entry by new competitors, and other factors. Management in such industries may enjoy a broad area of discretion as to how much profit to make. Since the managers, it is argued, derive no direct pecuniary benefit from higher profits, they can be expected to subordinate profit maximization to objectives of more immediate personal concern, such as security, corporate image, pleasant surrounding, good labor relations, high salaries, empire building, and so forth. Such tendencies should be especially pronounced among monopolists, since they enjoy the greatest freedom from competitive pressures. From this it might seem proper to infer that an unregulated monopolist would not charge monopoly prices or collect monopoly profits.

I consider this dubious reasoning. To begin with, the view that managers of a publicly held firm are likely to maximize stockholder earnings is at least as plausible as the view that they are not. Investors do care a great deal about the earnings of the firms in which they invest, since earnings significantly affect both dividends and the market value of a stock. Large investors, at least, do have ways of impressing their concerns on management. And the take-over bid is not unknown. It constitutes an ever-present threat to the incumbent management, and like any deterrent its effectiveness cannot be measured by the frequency with which it is actually employed. Moreover, most firms require access to outside capital as at least a marginal source of funds, and diminished earnings will mean diminished funds from the sale of additional securities. Even if not coerced by stockholders or market forces to maximize earnings, business managers might adopt that course because they viewed earnings as the most appropriate criterion of business success and the surest path to prestige, security, and other elements of personal fulfillment. Not least, managers typically do own stock in their company, not enough for control but quite enough to give them a substantial personal stake in the stock's performance and therefore in the firm's earnings.

The empirical evidence on profit maximization by large and relatively secure firms is as yet inconclusive. We know, for example, that patent and copyright holders and other monopolists commonly practice price discrimination.[8] As we shall soon see, discrimination is the profit-maximizing strategy of a monopolist. At the same time it is highly unpopular with purchasers, government agencies, and society at large. Its prevalence in these circumstances is some indication of the persistence of the profit drive among those insulated from direct competitive pressures. But it is an inconclusive indication. We shall soon see that price discrimination is consistent with other corporate goals besides maximizing the shareholders' earnings.

The evidence in support of the new theories of the firm is also impressionistic and inconclusive.[9] Perhaps the best evidence is the fact

[8]For examples of price discrimination by two unregulated monopolists, Alcoa (before World War II) and United Shoe Machinery, see C. KAYSEN, UNITED STATES V. UNITED SHOE MACHINERY CORPORATION: AN ECONOMIC ANALYSIS OF AN ANTI-TRUST CASE 146 (1956); Machlup, *Characteristics and Types of Price Discrimination,* in BUSINESS CONCENTRATION AND PRICE POLICY 397, 417–18 (Nat'l Bureau Econ. Research 1955).

[9]William Baumol characterizes the empirical basis for his theory that firms seek to maximize sales revenues rather than profits as "impressions gathered through casual observation." W. BAUMOL, BUSINESS BEHAVIOR, VALUE AND GROWTH 27 (rev. ed. 1967). Contrary evidence is not difficult to adduce at this level. The following is a quotation from the president of a large corporation: "'We are not interested in volume unless it is highly profitable. The name of the game used to be "how high do you stand on *Fortune's* 500." We've dropped from 393 to 481 in the past three years. But we have gone from a 64¢ a share loss before special items in 1965 to a 51¢ profit in 1967 by chopping off $30,000,000 worth of sales.'" INVESTOR'S READER, Sept. 4, 1968, at 17. Moreover, careful empirical study has failed to substantiate Baumol's hypothesis. *See, e.g.,* Mabry & Siders, *An Empirical Test of the Sales Maximization Hypothesis,* 33 S. ECON. J. 367 (1967). The case studies of O. WILLIAMSON, *supra* note 7, and of R. CYERT & J. MARCH, A BEHAVIORAL THEORY OF THE FIRM (1963), are suggestive but inconclusive. (Additional studies are summarized in Williamson, *A Dynamic Stochastic Theory of Managerial Behavior,* in PRICES: ISSUES IN THEORY, PRACTICE, AND PUBLIC POLICY 11, 22–23 (A. Phillips & O. Williamson eds. 1967). They show that under conditions of adversity firms find it possible to reduce costs appreciably. From this it is inferred that a firm not faced by adversity will allow a considerable organizational slack to build up despite the sacrifice of profits entailed thereby. But this is not a necessary inference. What is slack under adversity may be appropriate use of resources in other periods. When a firm's sales decline, for example, clearly it must adjust its expenses even though they were appropriate for the former level of output. For some recent statistical evidence that management-controlled firms may be less profitable than owner-controlled see Monsen, Chiu & Cooley, *The Effect of Separation of Ownership and Control in the Performance of the Large Firm,* 82 Q.J. ECON. 435 (1968).

that many corporations make charitable contributions. However, the amounts that corporations give to charity are trivial in relation to their profits,[10] and one of the reasons why this is so, surely, is that stockholders would be justifiably outraged to see management divert substantial profits, properly theirs, to charitable ends of the managers' devising. At most, such evidence indicates that firms do not always seek to maximize short-run profit when to do so might undermine the firm's prosperity in the long run. A charitable contribution is fully consistent with long-run profit maximization; a modest expenditure buys an asset of some value to any firm appraising its long-term prospects—public goodwill. The corporate-gift example suggests a reconciliation of the opposing viewpoints in the debate over profit maximization: the large corporation seeks to maximize profits, but over the long rather than the short run.[11]

A more critical point for our purposes is that even if the management of a monopolistic firm chooses not to maximize shareholder earnings—profits in the accounting sense—it might charge the same price that a conventional profit maximizer would charge, that is, the monopoly price. "Profit" and "profit maximization" are ambiguous concepts. To say that a firm is not maximizing profit may mean any one of a number of different things, and it is necessary to distinguish them. First, it may mean that the managers are, in effect, diverting monopoly profits to themselves in the form of salaries, bonuses, perquisites, and staff far in excess of what is required to attract and retain a competent management.[12] Such a course of action, if pursued by the management of a monopoly firm, would require the fixing of a monopoly price in order to support the abnormal return to the managers.

Second, insistent upon only moderate profit, the management of a monopolistic firm might be slack and allow costs to drift upward.

---

[10]*See* Hetherington, *Fact and Legal Theory: Shareholders, Managers, and Corporate Social Responsibility*, 21 STAN. L. REV. 248, 279 n. 103 (1969); Schwartz, *Corporate Philanthropic Contributions*, 23 J. FIN. 479 (1968).

[11]*Cf.* D. LAMBERTON, *supra* note 7, at 101–02; Mabry & Siders, *supra* note 9, at 377. As used in this context, the term "long run" does not have its usual connotation in economic discussion of a period within which all costs are variable; that is, long-lived assets wear out (or become obsolete) and must be replaced. The contrast I wish to suggest, rather, is between maximizing for all periods and maximizing only for the present period, or, less formally, between a time horizon of, say, 5–10 years and one of, say, 1–2 years.

[12]*See* O. WILLIAMSON, *supra* note 7, at 129–34.

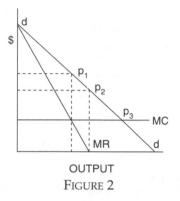

OUTPUT

FIGURE 2

This hypothesis also assumes that prices well above the minimum attainable cost level are being charged. Third, management might try to maximize profit but fail because of uncertainty about demand, costs, and other relevant conditions. Or, baffled by the complexities of determining the precise combination of outputs and prices that maximizes profit, management might fall back on more or less crude proxies or rules of thumb to guide its decision.[13] Presumably, however, its decision rules would be designed to approximate monopoly price.

It has also been suggested that management typically seeks to maximize sales revenues rather than profits, as an end in itself.[14] It is not clear, however, that a sales-maximizing monopoly would charge a price or prices that did not return substantial monopoly profits. This is best shown graphically (a procedure that has the added advantage of introducing some concepts that will recur in later discussion). Under the cost and demand conditions pictured in Figure 2, a profit-maximizing monopolist selling at a single price would sell at p_1. From any higher price (and therefore smaller output) the firm would have an incentive to move toward p_1; for an additional sale would generate more extra revenue (marginal revenue or MR) than

[13]See W. BAUMOL, *supra* note 9, at 29–30.

[14]W. BAUMOL, *supra* note 9, at 46–48. Professor Baumol also presents a modified version of the sales-maximization hypothesis: Companies seek to maximize the rate at which their sales *grow*. *Id.* at 96–101. This formulation is not entirely easy to distinguish from old-fashioned profit maximization, since, as Professor Baumol stresses (*id.* at 96–97), large profits are necessary to facilitate rapid corporate expansion and to attract such outside capital as is necessary to that end. *See also* R. MARRIS, THE ECONOMIC THEORY OF 'MANAGERIAL' CAPITALISM (1964).

11

extra cost (marginal cost or *MC*). A sales-maximizing monopolist, on the other hand, would sell at p_2. Any lower price would produce negative marginal revenue—that is, his total sales revenue would decline. Under competition, finally, price would be bid down to p_3, where price equals marginal cost. Thus, in our illustration the sales-maximizing price is well above the competitive price and includes substantial monopoly profits. But one should note that this is not a necessary characteristic of monopoly; if *MC* intersects *dd* at or above p_2, the sales-maximizing price will be equal to or lower than the competitive price.

Thus far, it has been assumed that a monopolist would sell at a single price. Figure 3 shows, however, that a profit-maximizing monopolist able to discriminate perfectly (we shall see later that natural monopolists are normally in a good position to discriminate finely, although not perfectly) will sell at the range of different prices lying along *dd* between *A* and *B* (the latter being the point at which *MC* intersects *dd*) and will obtain a monopoly profit of *ABC*. The sales-maximizing monopolist will proceed likewise but will then continue down the demand curve, selling additional output at prices ranging from *B* down to a point just above *E*, and will thereby obtain additional revenue *BEF* (at a loss equal to *BDE*).

From a monopolist's decision to maximize sales, therefore, it does not necessarily follow that he will not obtain monopoly returns. A final possibility is that management might, out of pure benignity, forgo any monopoly profit and sell at the same price that competition would dictate. But there is no evidence that such a tendency is common, and it would be surprising if it were. In sum, unless this

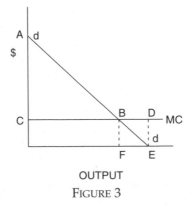

OUTPUT

FIGURE 3

last and least plausible version of the revisionist theory is adopted, even a "non-profit-maximizing" monopolist is quite likely to charge the monopoly rather than the competitive price.[15] The relationship between the profit motive and pricing policy is loose in another respect. A price that does not maximize profit may be either lower or higher than the profit-maximizing price, and if it is higher the impact on efficient resource allocation will be even more adverse than if the firm charged the profit-maximizing price.

The controversy over whether firms insulated from strong competitive pressure maximize profit thus sheds little light on monopoly pricing. On the other hand, the distinction mentioned earlier between short-run and long-run profit maximization is highly pertinent. Business policies designed to maximize the present period's earnings may be short-sighted in their neglect of events that could drastically impair future profits, such as restrictive legislation or entry by new competitors into the firm's markets. A monopolist maximizing long-run profit may or may not charge the monopoly price determined without regard for more or less distant contingencies. On the one hand, he may decide to sell at a somewhat lower price in order to discourage entry by potential competitors or for other strategic reasons.[16] On the other hand, he may charge the monopoly price but divert a portion of the abnormal return to expenditures designed to improve the firm's long-run position. An example would be an ad-

---

[15]Whether monopoly profit is taken directly or transformed into unnecessary expenses (*e.g.*, slack) will not affect monopoly pricing but may affect other dimensions of the monopoly problem. Thus, diversion to workers of monopoly profit in the form of an excessively generous wage settlement does not detract from the inefficiency of the firm's charging a monopoly price, but it does mitigate distributive inequality, since presumably workers, unlike stockholders, are not as a group richer than consumers. On the general subject of the pricing implications of various theories of the firm see Williamson, *supra* note 9.

[16]Alcoa apparently followed a policy of limit pricing when it had a monopoly of aluminum production. *See* United States v. Aluminum Co. of America, 148 F.2d 416, 426 (2d Cir. 1945). *See also* M. BOWMAN & G. BACH, ECONOMIC ANALYSIS AND PUBLIC POLICY 388–89 (2d ed. 1949); Coase, *Some Notes on Monopoly Price*, 5 REV. ECON. STUDIES 17, 26 (1937). For other strategic considerations supporting self-restraint in pricing see W. BAUMOL, *supra* note 9, at 43, 46. One might ask why entry would not be as effectively deterred simply by the knowledge that the monopolist could, if threatened by new entry, reduce his price, and therefore why limit pricing is a rational strategy. A possible answer is that in contemplating entry a firm is more likely to look to the price being charged in the market than to the costs of the firms selling there, because it is ordinarily much easier for a firm to determine the price charged by, than the costs of, another firm.

vertising campaign designed to generate public goodwill (rather than to expand sales) in order to ward off possible political interference with the continued enjoyment by the firm of its monopoly position, or, as previously mentioned, a charitable contribution designed with a similar effect in mind.

To summarize our discussion of profit maximization, the traditional assumption that a monopolist will strive to charge the monopoly price remains quite plausible, subject to one important qualification: The monopoly price depends on management's time horizon. In the long run, a persistently very large spread between price and cost may spur entrepreneurs to devise ingenious methods of challenging or supplanting the monopolist and legislatures of curbing him. The long-run monopoly price—a price fixed with these dangers in mind—may thus be significantly lower than the short-run monopoly price, although still well above cost. There is at least this much validity to the revisionist view of the modern corporation: It is plausible to suppose that the management of a typical monopolist would identify its own interests with the long-run interests of the corporation and would have sufficient independence from stockholders to fix the long-run monopoly price without fear of being dislodged. Although no more than plausible, this theory does have some empirical support.[17]

Let us turn now to a second respect on which the conventional assumption that monopoly results in excessive prices requires not contradiction but careful qualification. It is this: In attempting to determine the degree to which monopoly prices can reasonably be deemed excessive, it is improper to compare returns under monopoly with returns under fully competitive conditions. Competitive returns may no longer be the norm in our economy, given the prevalence[18] of oligopoly. Many economists believe that firms in an oligopolistic market, a market in which a few firms account for most sales, tend to avoid vigorous price competition. Each one realizes that a price cut by it will cut so deeply into the sales of the others as to evoke prompt matching responses, resulting in lower profits for

[17]Studies of the pre-World War II Alcoa monopoly offer some support. *See* United States v. Aluminum Co. of America, 148 F.2d 416, 426 (2d Cir. 1945); L. WEISS, ECONOMICS AND AMERICAN INDUSTRY 221–22 (1961). *But cf.* D. WALLACE, MARKET CONTROL IN THE ALUMINUM INDUSTRY 225–63 (1937).

[18]*See* J. BAIN, INDUSTRIAL ORGANIZATION 133–49 (2d ed. 1968); C. KAYSEN & D. TURNER, ANTITRUST POLICY 26–41 (1959).

all.[19] No economist believes that the number of firms in a market is the only index to whether such behavior is likely; for example, unless entry is for some reason difficult, tacit collusion to maintain a supra-competitive price level by the existing firms in the market, however few they may be, is unlikely to succeed for very long. Nor is it at all clear how concentrated a market must be for oligopolistic interdependence to emerge. But it is at least plausible that in many, perhaps most, markets today the pattern of prices and profits lies somewhere between that of monopoly and that of competition—and perhaps closer to the former than to the latter in a nontrivial number of cases—due to oligopoly.

Even so, one might reply, the proper course would be to restructure oligopolistic markets where necessary to restore competitive conditions and to force the prices of natural monopolists down to the competitive level through regulation; and if restructuring is impossible there is still no reason to allow the natural monopolist to earn more than a competitive return. Such reasoning raises some serious questions. Although this is not the place to explore the matter in detail, it is not clear that a broad restructuring of oligopolistic markets would be justified. To penalize by dissolution firms that succeed in obtaining large market shares could have a very bad effect on the incentive to compete aggressively. Moreover, the implementation of a policy of restructuring would probably be costly and prolonged. An administrative or judicial determination would have to be made of the minimum firm size[20] in each market; even in theory, this is an exceedingly difficult determination to make.[21] These objections are weighty because the benefits of restructuring are somewhat speculative. There is considerable uncertainty about the actual effect of oligopoly on pricing. Conceivably it is not very great.[22]

If we assume, for these or other reasons, that our economy is likely to remain highly oligopolistic (a stiff law prohibiting mergers that

[19]This assumes that demand for the firms' product is neither growing rapidly nor highly sensitive to price decreases. If either condition holds, all of the firms may be better off at a lower price level.

[20]*Not* plant size, because there may be substantial multiplant economies to single-firm operation—for example, in marketing.

[21]*See generally* Stigler, *The Economies of Scale,* 1 J. LAW & ECON. 54 (1958), *reprinted in* G. STIGLER, THE ORGANIZATION OF INDUSTRY 71 (1968).

[22]*See* Stigler, *A Theory of Oligopoly,* 72 J. POL. ECON. 44 (1964), *reprinted in* G. STIGLER, *supra* note 21, at 39. *But see, e.g.,* N. COLLINS & L. PRESTON, CONCENTRATION AND PRICE-COST MARGINS IN MANUFACTURING INDUSTRIES 115–16 (1968).

15

contribute to market concentration has been on the books for 18 years now without perceptibly reducing the degree of concentration),[23] there are compelling reasons for not attempting to reduce a natural monopolist's profit below whatever is the prevailing level in such an economy. It would be a curious policy that devoted substantial resources to compressing profits to the competitive level in a relatively small sector of the economy while countenancing in a much larger sector profits that may be substantially supracompetitive. Such special treatment could not be justified by any difference in the importance of the services provided by natural monopolists. What could be more vital than drugs and medicines, currently produced by a highly oligopolistic industry that enjoys an exceptionally high profit level?[24]

In addition, to eliminate prices that exceed competitive levels in one industry while tolerating their continuance in many others is inefficient; it will cause excessive migration of resources to the former. Consumers will buy more of the product because the cost to them is now reduced, even though a substitute product made by another industry meets the same need better and at lower cost to society. From the standpoint of efficient allocation, a more sensible objective for an economy permeated by excessive returns may be to proportionalize the excess-profit factor in the prices of goods and services so as not to distort consumer choice (though even this is subject to a number of qualifications). But whatever may be the "second best" solution when the best (all prices at competitive levels) is unattainable, it is not to eliminate profits lopsidedly and thereby create improper price signals.[25]

---

[23]*Hearings on the Status and Future of Small Business in the American Economy Before the Senate Comm. on Small Business,* 90th Cong., 1st Sess. 475, 484 (1967) (statement of Dr. Willard F. Mueller, Director, Bureau of Economics, Federal Trade Commission). The law, of course, is the Celler-Kefauver Antimerger Act, amending section 7 of the Clayton Act, 15 U.S.C. § 18 (1964).

[24]Profits after taxes of more than 20 percent of stockholders' equity are not uncommon. Merck, for example, had a 25.4 percent profit in 1967. FORTUNE, June 15, 1968, at 192–93.

[25]For discussions of the vexing problem of "second best" solutions to allocative inefficiency see 2 J. MEADE, THEORY OF INTERNATIONAL ECONOMIC POLICY 102–18 (1955); Baumol, *Monopolistic Competition and Welfare Economics,* 54 AM. ECON. REV. PAPERS & PROCEEDINGS 44, 46 (1964); Lipsey & Lancaster, *The General Theory of Second Best,* 24 REV. ECON. STUDIES 11, 16–17, 25 (1956); Mishan, *Second Thoughts on Second Best,* 14 OXFORD ECON. PAPERS (N.S.) 205, 214–17 (1962).

One would not be concerned with the allocative consequences of forcing down a monopolist's price to marginal cost when other products were being sold at prices in

Nevertheless, it is probably the case that unregulated natural monopolists could extract profits somewhat higher than those prevailing in oligopolistic industries; and to eliminate *that* excess might well be a step in the right direction. As noted earlier, the precise impact of oligopoly on price competition is not known and may not be very great after all, especially in the many industries that are only loosely oligopolistic in structure. And oligopolists lack the advantage over potential competitors that the natural monopolist has by virtue of the economies of scale in a natural monopoly market. The monopoly return might, consequently, be higher than one would judge desirable. But the magnitude is uncertain. Moreover, so long as oligopolistic interdependence, governmentally sanctioned restrictive practices (as in agriculture), and other serious market imperfections result in substantial disparities between price and marginal cost in *some* important markets not wholly unrelated to the natural monopoly markets, we cannot be *sure* that the elimination of monopoly pricing in the latter markets would improve the efficient allocation of resources or even that it would not worsen it. Analysis of the "second best" problem has demonstrated the pitfalls of the piecemeal approach.

Finally, one should note that the possession of a monopoly does not always enable a firm to charge the monopoly price. Although only a single natural gas pipeline company can efficiently supply a new increment of demand in the Los Angeles retail market (let us say), more than one pipeline company in the western United States is in a position to construct and operate that pipeline. The retail gas company serving the Los Angeles market can therefore (I am assuming no regulatory constraints on the bargaining process) invite bids from several competitors for the opportunity to serve that market. Unless the bidding process is collusive, the pipeline that wins the long-term contract to supply the city's new demand should be the one whose price for the term is closest to cost and contains the least monopoly profit.[26] But the bargaining process cannot be relied upon as a complete solution to the problem of monopoly price. Unless the

---

excess of their marginal costs if there were no substitutes for the monopolist's product. There would in that case be no allocative consequences. But if monopoly markets are that insulated from other markets, neither is there any reason to expect that monopoly pricing has any misallocative effects, *i.e.*, that it shifts demand to substitutes that cost society more to produce.

[26]*See* Demsetz, *Why Regulate Utilities?*, 11 J. LAW & ECON. 55 (1968); *cf.* United States v. El Paso Natural Gas Co., 376 U.S. 651 (1964).

parties build in private regulatory devices such as renegotiation with arbitration in the event of disagreement, the process may create an inefficient bias toward contract terms longer than risk conditions justify. More important, the buying side may be too fragmented to bargain effectively (as is true of telephone subscribers, for example). Still, bargaining may be an antidote to monopoly pricing in some cases, and it is an especially significant factor to be borne in mind when contemplating the extension of regulation to a new industry such as cable television, where the opportunity of local government, representing the subscribers, to drive a hard bargain with the would-be monopolist may be a viable alternative to conventional methods of regulation.[27]

Admitting the force of the foregoing points, it is nonetheless plausible to assume that an unregulated monopolist will typically set prices and obtain profits that are in a meaningful sense excessive, albeit less so than popularly supposed. But it is a fair question whether the eradication of such excess profits is necessary or important to the social goals of promoting equitable income distribution, overall economic stability, efficient allocation of resources, and incentives to innovation and cost reduction.

Society condemns certain forms of income redistribution because of the means employed and without inquiry into the impact of the redistribution on the pattern of incomes; an extreme example is larceny. The first question in evaluating the distributive effect of unregulated natural monopoly, therefore, is whether the natural monopolist's extraction of consumers' surplus is the kind of conduct that should be prevented regardless of the actual magnitude or direction of its effect on incomes. If the answer is no, we proceed to the next question, whether unregulated natural monopoly causes or contributes to a socially undesirable income distribution.

In considering the first question we may begin by noting that a monopoly profit is simply a form of "economic rent," a term economists apply to any return obtained by virtue of controlling a scarce or unique factor of production. The profit that an individual realizes when he sells his home in an area where the pressure of increasing population has made real estate more scarce and therefore more valuable than when he bought is a classic example of economic rent. While the receipt of economic rents was once a burning social

[27]*See* text accompanying notes 199–201 *infra*.

18

issue in America,[28] it is no longer. The conventional reply to a comparison of monopoly to other rents is that monopoly rents are the result of an artificial, contrived scarcity rather than a natural scarcity, and that prices inflated by a rent factor serve a valuable purpose in rationing naturally scarce resources such as land or petroleum while the monopolist's rents serve no comparable social purpose. The reply is compelling if one's image of the monopolist is of the classical "engrosser" who buys up all of the available corn on the way to the market and then forces up the price by withholding an adequate supply, or of the holder of a government franchise that limits entry of competitors. Our concern is with the unregulated *natural* monopolist. His market power flows from the cost and demand characteristics of the market in which he is selling, rather than from unfair or restrictive tactics or from legal privileges. Moreover, we shall see that the natural monopolist is well situated to adopt a method of pricing—discrimination—that maximizes profit without necessarily restricting output.[29] Thus, although a natural monopolist should be able to extract large profits, it is difficult from an ethical standpoint to distinguish an individual who obtains a high return by virtue of an interest in a natural monopoly firm from one who owns a strategically located plot of land and watches its value rise year after year without any skill or effort on his part.

Neither is it true that monopoly profits, unlike other forms of economic rent, serve no useful function in the regulation of the economy, although the function they serve is not rationing. Under competition, we need worry little about a firm's incentives to price efficiently, to minimize its costs, and to innovate. If it is inefficient the firm may be badly hurt or even destroyed by its rivals; the possibility should provide enough motivation for good performance. The "stick" of competitive displacement is absent under monopoly, or at least smaller. But supracompetitive profits provide a substitute incentive that may be nearly as effective, although in the form of a "car-

[28]For the story of Henry George's crusade against land rents see H. GEORGE, PROGRESS AND POVERTY (1954); 3 J. DORFMAN, THE ECONOMIC MIND IN AMERICAN CIVILIZATION 142–49 (1949).

[29]*See* text accompanying notes 43–47 *infra*. One should note, however, that to effectuate price discrimination a monopolist may have to impose on his purchaser restrictions against resale, in which event he would be interfering with the workings of a free market. But we shall see that such restrictions are typically not necessary in natural monopoly markets because the product is a service, which by nature is not readily transferable.

rot." To anticipate subsequent discussion, the unregulated monopolist has a strong incentive to price efficiently, to minimize costs, and to innovate, because these tactics will enable him to increase his profits. Deny the monopolist the opportunity to obtain profits in excess of his costs and you may destroy his incentive to better his performance. In principle, one would like to distinguish between those supracompetitive profits that reward a monopolist for superior performance and those that constitute a simple mulcting of the consumer. In practice such a separation seems impossible.[30]

Our comparison of land and natural monopoly rents suggests a general formulation of the difference between redistributions that are condemned regardless of their actual effect on the pattern of incomes in society and those that are condoned unless that effect is harmful. Some activities are, at best, worthless to society. Examples are the manufacture of burglary tools and the formation and enforcement of cartels. These activities are to be discouraged quite apart from any effect on income distribution. It is thus sufficient condemnation of the redistributions to which burglary or the monopolization of competitive markets gives rise that they constitute inducements to socially undesirable conduct.[31] But the effort of a businessman to monopolize a market by producing at a cost so low as to drive out his competitors and deter new entry or, the monopoly achieved, to improve his return by lowering his costs still further is not at all reprehensible.[32] It is conduct we want to encourage, and supracompetitive profits provide the inducement to engage in it. While, to repeat, it would be nice to be able to distinguish between those supracompetitive profits that provide the necessary inducement to efficiency and those that are pure windfalls, in the absence of a reliable method for making the distinction it is unreasonable to equate the profits of natural monopoly with those of antisocial conduct.

The remaining question is whether the profits of natural monopolists cause or aggravate an undesirable pattern of incomes in society. To answer this question, we must first determine what the income ef-

[30]See text accompanying notes 175–84 infra. The term "monopoly profits" will be used throughout to embrace both kinds of supracompetitive return.

[31]See Tullock, The Welfare Costs of Tariffs, Monopolies and Theft, 5 W. ECON. J. 224 (1967).

[32]One could, of course, argue that the opportunity to reap natural monopoly profits may bias private inventive activity in the direction of process or product innovations that lend themselves to monopolistic exploitation because they involve large economies of scale.

20

fect of monopoly profits is. The conventional assumption that they redistribute income from a poorer class—consumers—to a richer—stockholders—cannot be maintained without careful qualification. On the consumer side of the equation, one should note that many purchasers of natural monopoly services are business firms, which sometimes will, but sometimes will not, be able to pass on the bulk of a cost increase to *their* customers. At some point, moreover, many of the "essential" services provided under conditions of natural monopoly become luxuries. Examples are colored telephones, water for swimming pools, electricity for air conditioning, and long-distance telephony for casual chit-chat. Stated another way, natural monopoly services seem to some extent income elastic: Wealthier people tend to buy more and poorer less of these services. A profit-maximizing monopolist in these circumstances will try to design a rate schedule that enables the poorer consumer to purchase at a price closer to the marginal cost of serving him than the wealthier consumer is charged, lest the former be deterred from taking service by a high price. Since, as explained later, a natural monopolist's marginal cost is lower than his average total cost, this kind of price discrimination—discrimination in favor of the less affluent and against the more affluent consumer—may in some instances enable the less affluent to obtain natural monopoly services at lower rates than those corresponding to average total cost. Competition, if it were viable under these conditions, would prevent the seller from loading a disproportionate amount of his total costs on a group of wealthier customers able and, in the absence of good substitutes, willing to shoulder them;[33] it would force him to charge everybody average total cost.[34]

[33]For a fuller discussion of price discrimination by natural monopolists see text accompanying notes 43–49 *infra*.

[34]A further point is that the creation of a natural monopoly will—paradoxically—usually make the consumer better off than he was before, even if he must pay a very high monopoly price. Most natural monopolies have arisen not from changes in the methods of producing existing products or services but from the creation of new services—such as telegraphy, telephony, and electric power. The cost of a new service to the consumer, including whatever monopoly profit the seller is able to include, must be lower than that of the service it displaced; otherwise it would not have displaced the old service. But perhaps the proper comparison is not between today's consumers and yesterday's but among present-day consumers. Also, one should note that the displacement of an existing by a new service may harm some consumers—those who preferred the former service but could not sustain it by themselves when most of their fellow consumers switched to the new.

On the shareholder side of the redistribution equation, one should note that a significant proportion of the equity capital in our society is owned by employee pension funds, by universities and other charitable foundations, and by individuals of moderate means.[35] Some monopoly profits, moreover, are probably distributed to individuals other than shareholders—for example to workers.[36] Most important, the degree to which wealthy individuals can actually increase their wealth by virtue of monopoly profits depends critically on the structure of the tax laws. To illustrate, let us suppose that company X, in a competitive market, has net income of $200,000 per year before federal corporate income tax. To simplify computation the tax will be assumed to be a flat 50 percent. Company X's net income after tax will therefore be $100,000. Assume that the market value of its common stock is $2 million, all owned by individuals in the 70 percent bracket of the federal personal income tax, and that X distributes 50 percent of its after tax income as dividends. Suppose that X obtains a monopoly of its market, and is able to increase its net income before tax by, say, 50 percent, or $100,000. Since one-half of the additional income is taxed away by the corporation tax, X's net income after tax will increase to $150,000.

The stockholders will not be greatly enriched by the added dividends—$25,000—that accrue to them annually as a result of the acquisition of a monopoly, because $17,500 will be taxed away. They will be enriched for another reason. Assuming that the price-earnings ratio before the monopoly was acquired remains unchanged (for reasons that we need not dwell on here, it might well be higher or lower), the market value of X common stock will rise from $2 to $3 million. If the stockholders (all of whom, we shall assume, have owned the stock for more than six months) sell their shares at the new price, they will realize a gain of $1 million, of which only $250,000 will be taxed away. Although they will not, of course, re-

---

[35]At the end of 1967, pension funds and nonprofit institutions held roughly 12 percent (by market value) of the stock listed on the New York Stock Exchange, and mutual insurance and savings institutions held additional substantial amounts. Computed from NEW YORK STOCK EXCHANGE, 1968 FACT BOOK 42 (1968). More than 50 percent of the shareholders of public corporations had a reported household income of less than $10,000 per year. Computed from NEW YORK STOCK EXCHANGE, 1965 CENSUS OF SHAREOWNERS 15 (1965). On the other hand, all but 3 percent of the corporate stock (by market value) owned by consumer units in this country in 1962 was owned by the wealthiest 20 percent of those units. INEQUALITY AND POVERTY xxii (E. Budd ed. 1967).

[36]See note 15 supra and text accompanying note 52 infra.

ceive the added dividends that they would have received had they kept the stock, $7,500 per year after taxes is obviously a poor swap for a lump sum after taxes of $750,000.

What is involved here is a gaping loophole in the federal personal income tax that enables individuals largely to escape the progressive feature of the tax by capitalizing future earnings. Were there no difference in treatment between long-term capital gains and other income, the principal beneficiary of monopoly profits would be the United States Government. Presumably revenues from this source would be expended by the government in accordance with public needs, including that of distributive justice.

In sum, if the tax system were really designed to further distributive justice, the distributive effect of monopoly as of other profits would be adequately corrected; as discussed earlier, there is no reason to draw invidious distinctions between natural monopoly and other forms of rent or income. If, on the other hand, the tax system is unprogressive, special treatment of the profits of natural monopolists will do little to achieve social justice. The natural monopoly sector is a small part of the economy.[37] The opportunities for altering the distribution of wealth by profit maximization in that sector pale by comparison with those afforded by the long-term capital-gains and other tax loopholes. And if special treatment of natural monopoly profits is nevertheless desired, we shall see that it can quite possibly be achieved by minor modification of the tax laws at less social cost than by a system of direct regulatory controls.[38]

One can question, finally, whether income equalization is sound social policy, at least in the sense that would justify efforts to eliminate natural monopoly profits.[39] Most contemporary economists, for

[37]In 1967 the percentage of Gross National Product contributed by electrical, gas, telephone, and water companies, the principal natural monopolists, was well under 5. Railroads provided another 1.2 percent. Computed from United States Department of Commerce, Office of Business Economics, 48 SURVEY OF CURRENT BUSINESS, July 1968, at 27.

[38]See text accompanying note 196 infra.

[39]For a variety of perspectives relevant to the general question of distributive justice, see INEQUALITY AND POVERTY (E. Budd 1967); R. DAHL & C. LINDBLOM, POLITICS, ECONOMICS, AND WELFARE 134–61 (1953); G. KOLKO, WEALTH AND POWER IN AMERICA—AN ANALYSIS OF SOCIAL CLASS AND INCOME DISTRIBUTION (1962); A. LERNER, THE ECONOMICS OF CONTROL: PRINCIPLES OF WELFARE ECONOMICS 23–40 (1944); R. MUSGRAVE, THE THEORY OF PUBLIC FINANCE: A STUDY IN PUBLIC ECONOMY 19–22, 98–110 (1959); P. SAMUELSON, FOUNDATIONS OF ECONOMIC ANALYSIS 243–49 (1947); T. SCITOVSKY, supra note 6; Rahl, Distributive Justice, in PHILOSOPHY, POLITICS AND SOCIETY—THIRD SERIES 58 (P. Laslett & W. Runciman eds. 1967).

example, would be unwilling to assert that a more equal distribution of wealth would increase the sum of human welfare or happiness. One can, to be sure, imagine cases where a redistribution from a wealthier to a poorer individual probably would increase the well-being of the latter more than it diminished the well-being of the former: A dime is doubtless worth more to a beggar than to most millionaires. But if we ask whether a redistribution of $1,000 in annual income from a family whose income is $20,000 to a family whose income is $10,000 would have a similar effect, we shall indicate the difficulty of making interpersonal comparisons of utility, except in extreme cases. Not only do individuals with larger incomes tend to have larger expenses and a different conception of what is a necessity and what a luxury, but a higher income may compensate for the absence of nonmonetary satisfactions (such as greater leisure or less responsibility) that a lower-paying occupation might yield.

A theory having greater intuitive appeal is that the individual from whom wealth is redistributed (whether he is more or less affluent) will usually feel a sense of loss that is greater than the recipient's sense of gain—that people value the wealth they have more than new increments. This theory, however, lends little support to a policy of eliminating natural monopoly profits. We noted earlier that conditions of natural monopoly are historically associated with the creation of new services.[40] A consumer will not patronize a new service unless it makes him better off to do so, and if it does, he will not feel that his wealth has diminished even if the price of the new service includes a substantial monopoly profit.

The utilitarian ethic, then, the ethic that underlies the economist's conception of social welfare, does not imply a goal of equalizing incomes, save perhaps to the extent necessary to eliminate the extreme inequality we call poverty. On the contrary, the economist would be concerned, and rightly so, with the possible social cost in reduced incentives of equalizing the rewards of economic activity, not to mention the possible diminution in human satisfaction that might result from forced income uniformity among individuals of widely different tastes and ambitions. Since welfare economics is not the only source of social values, we cannot end our inquiry here. But other normative systems appear to yield a similar answer. Contemporary conceptions of fairness and social justice may be thought to require

[40]*See* note 34 *supra.*

24

that the community assure all individuals the monetary resources necessary to maintain a decent minimum level of existence. And one can bolster this ethical notion with the political scientists' perception that poverty breeds social unrest and with the economists' that poverty has harmful spillover effects on the rest of society, for example, in the form of higher crime rates. It is also possible that extreme concentrations of wealth are a threat to political stability. What is elusive is any broader goal of income equality than that implied by the preceding discussion. Certainly it is not to be found in the traditional American ideal of equality of economic *opportunity*, which is not at all the same thing as equality of economic rewards. Equality of rewards seems, if anything, inconsistent with equality of opportunity, and with other basic values such as personal freedom and individualism.

Less abstractly, in a society that is generally affluent even wide disparities of income may be quite tolerable, and necessary to foster individual incentive. The distributive objective in such a society shifts from greater equality of incomes as such to closing the gap between the majority of people, who are reasonably well off, and the minority who do not share in the general affluence. The income disparities that trouble our society today are not between individuals who have large unearned incomes and the rest of us, but between the average middle-class American and individuals who live in poverty. This points up the irrelevance of control of monopoly profits to any currently significant goal of income equalization. Redistribution of the profits of natural monopoly to consumers would alleviate the burdens of poverty to only a trivial extent. Unregulated land rents almost certainly are a much greater factor in the plight of the poor.

The reader might object that the foregoing critique of distributive justice undermines progressive taxation as well as control of monopoly profits. But that would be an erroneous inference. The Government must raise money somehow, and it is difficult to conceive of a method of doing so that would not have some effect on the distribution of income. In a context where distributive effects are probably unavoidable, it may be appropriate to indulge a preference for equality—though how far, and indeed whether income taxation is the best method of doing so, are matters of legitimate debate. What emerges from our discussion is the absence of any tenable principle upon which to base special measures to alter the distribution of wealth as between a natural monopolist and its customers.

25

Concern with the impact of natural monopoly on economic stability also seems misplaced. Apart from the fact that the federal government has powerful weapons in its monetary and fiscal policies for preventing depressions or recessions, assuring full employment, and curbing excessive inflation, the natural monopoly markets are probably much too small a sector of the economy to affect overall stability materially. An increase in price and constriction of output in one market by reason of a changeover from competition to monopoly should cause an expansion of output and decrease in price in others. Workers would flow from the monopoly to competitive markets. Since the market price of the monopolist's stock would be bid up, so that subsequent purchasers obtained only a normal return, fears of excessive savings by wealthy shareholders seem exaggerated. If the monopolist responded to a general decline in consumer demand by raising his price still further, prices in competitive markets would simply decline more rapidly than would otherwise be the case. In short, so long as the natural monopoly markets remain a small sector of the economy, neither the formation nor subsequent behavior of natural monopolies is likely to aggravate business cycles significantly even in the absence of effective countercyclical policies.[41]

The argument that monopoly prices lead to a misallocation of resources requires qualification in three respects. First, as mentioned earlier it is difficult to assert confidently that the correction of excessive prices in one area of the economy will actually improve the efficiency of resource allocation; it may have the opposite effect. Second, some studies (contradicted, however, by others) indicate that the impact of allocative inefficiency on the nation's productivity may be slight, even if large monopoly profits are assumed.[42] Third, the theory is based on an assumption that is peculiarly vulnerable as applied to a natural monopoly. It is that the seller will charge a single price. As pointed out earlier, the reason why a monopolist, in order to maximize profit, must fix a price that excludes consumers perfectly willing to pay him a normal profit and more is that there is no single price that captures the entire consumers' surplus, individual

---

[41]See J. BAIN, PRICE THEORY 238–40 (1952); Stigler, *Administered Prices and Oligopolistic Inflation*, 35 J. Bus. U. CHI. I, 8–9 (1962), *reprinted in* G. STIGLER, *supra* note 21, at 235.

[42]See W. BAUMOL, WELFARE ECONOMICS AND THE THEORY OF THE STATE 101 (2d ed. 1965); Leibenstein, *Allocative Efficiency vs. "X-Efficiency,"* 56 AM. ECON. REV. 392–97 (1966), and studies cited therein. *But see* Kamerschen, *An Estimation of the "Welfare Losses" from Monopoly in the American Economy*, 4 W. ECON. J. 221 (1966).

consumers having different utility functions.[43] Suppose that the monopolist is not required to charge a single price but is free to charge different prices for the same product regardless of cost, and that his purchasers are unable to resell. In that event the profit-maximizing monopolist will want to charge each consumer who will pay, at a minimum, a price that returns the monopolist a normal or competitive profit (below which the monopolist could employ his resources more profitably elsewhere) as much as the particular consumer, considering his individual needs and alternatives, is willing to pay.[44] The widget example shows that this is indeed the profit-maximizing strategy. By charging 7 cents for the first 10,000 widgets, 6 cents for the next 2,000, 5 cents for the next 1,000, and 4 cents for the last 1,000, the monopolist obtains a monopoly profit of $350. Were he required to charge a single price to all purchasers, his maximum monopoly profit, as we saw earlier, would be only $300.

Not only is price discrimination the profit-maximizing strategy of a monopolist, but under conditions of natural monopoly it may be the only feasible method of pricing consistent with an efficient allocation of resources. Natural monopoly refers to a market whose entire demand can be met at lowest cost by a single firm. This implies that before a firm can begin to do business it must sink large sums in a plant that is large enough or can readily be expanded to serve the entire market. Once the heavy initial fixed or overhead expenses are incurred, the cost of serving a particular customer is relatively slight. If the firm charged every customer the cost of employing idle capacity to produce an additional unit of output, it would not recover its overhead costs. Faced with such a situation, the firm could charge a single price that included a proportional share of the overhead costs as well as the additional cost of producing the unit. But such pricing would violate efficient allocation. It would exclude customers perfectly willing and able to pay the actual cost of expanding production to meet their demands, but no more. One solution, perhaps efficient but surely unrealistic, is for the government to pay the firm a subsidy enabling it to charge *all* purchasers the cost of producing an additional unit. Another efficient—and more realistic—solution is dis-

---

[43]*See* text accompanying note 6 *supra.*

[44]Discrimination may also take the form of charging a customer different prices for different quantities of the good or service in question, since the strength of the purchaser's demand may vary with the quantity taken.

crimination. Those who will pay only the additional cost are charged that amount. Other purchasers are charged as much as they will pay. In this manner the monopolist can recover its total costs without turning away anyone willing to pay the minimum cost of producing the units that he takes.[45]

To illustrate, let us suppose that coal is discovered at Coaltown, 200 miles from the nearest market for coal (Markettown). Railroad R builds a line to Coaltown and fixes a rate (we shall assume no regulation) that covers both the total costs of the rail line—that is, the fixed costs (interest on bonds, real estate taxes, etc.) that are incurred regardless of whether any coal is actually hauled plus the expenses involved in the hauling—and the additional value that the coal operators, considering alternative transportation means and the price at which they can sell coal, are willing to pay the railroad to carry their product. Fixed costs are $10,000 a year, operating expenses $10 per ton, and the monopoly profit the railroad is able to exact $5 per ton. The railroad hauls 1,000 tons of coal from Coaltown each year. Since it averages the fixed costs over this quantity, the rate is $25 per ton.

The next year a lumber mill is built midway between Coaltown and Markettown. Because the lumber mill can truck its lumber products to Markettown for $17.51 per ton, it will not pay R $25. In these circumstances R, if sensible, will offer to carry the lumber mill's products for $17.50. At that price R covers the additional cost of serving this new customer ($10, since the coal operators are defraying the entire fixed costs of the line) and obtains a monopoly profit of $7.50.

Some years later a competing railroad, R', builds a line to Coaltown and offers to carry coal to Markettown for $12.51. Should R meet that rate or abandon the line? It should meet the rate. If the lumber mill is providing it with 1,000 tons of business a year, then at a rate of $12.50 to the coal operators and $17.50 to the lumber mill R will cover its total costs ($10,000 plus $10 per ton). Even if the lumber mill yields a smaller volume, so that R cannot cover its total costs at any price it can exact, it should not abandon the line, since both rates cover variable costs[46] and make some contribution to fixed or over-

[45]There is a good discussion of these points in Henderson, *The Pricing of Public Utility Undertakings,* 15 MANCHESTER SCHOOL OF ECON. & SOCIAL STUDIES 223 (1947). For a more recent treatment see Vickrey, *Some Implications of Marginal Cost Pricing for Public Utilities,* 55 AM. ECON. REV. PAPERS & PROCEEDINGS 605 (1965).

[46]Much "value of service" pricing in the regulated industries fails to do this. *See, e.g.,* J. MEYER, M. PECK, J. STENASON & C. ZWICK, THE ECONOMICS OF COMPETITION IN THE

head costs. Fixed costs—those incurred independently of actual operations—by definition cannot be avoided by a cessation of operations. The railroad would be worse off by abandonment, since it would continue to owe the full $10,000 a year.

The salient point is that the prices are efficient even though the price differential favoring the coal operators is not nicely proportionate to the cost of service (the lumber yard is closer and was established after the railroad incurred its heavy fixed costs in establishing the line to Coaltown, yet pays more) but only to the differing values that the respective customers place on the service. No customer willing to pay the minimum cost of serving him is denied service. And that was true when the price differential went the other way and both prices included substantial (but different) monopoly profits. A monopolist able to discriminate perfectly will not include in his price a monopoly profit so large that he will lose the customer.

Unhappily for efficiency (if not for other social values), perfect price discrimination is rarely possible. A monopolist ordinarily cannot bargain with or otherwise ascertain the demand elasticity of each potential customer for each individual unit of output; and if he could society might find the procedure intolerable because of its extortionate flavor. As a practical matter, the monopolist must establish classifications, and unless these are very fine, in the process of attempting to maximize his profits from each class he may end up restricting output by as much as—or even more than—he would have done by selling at a single price.[47] To be sure, since natural monopolists are typically sellers of services that can be metered and are not readily transferable, they should be able to practice a highly refined, although not perfect, form of discrimination. And intuitively one would suppose that a highly refined discriminatory pricing system would result in greater output than if the single monopoly price were charged. This may be true but it cannot be proved rigorously. We can say only that the output of a discriminating natural monopolist will not necessarily be suboptimal, and that the degree to which it is suboptimal will vary from market to market.

TRANSPORTATION INDUSTRIES 182 (1959). For discriminatory pricing to be efficient, the price to the favored purchaser must not be less than the true cost of serving him.

[47]*See* J. ROBINSON, THE ECONOMICS OF IMPERFECT COMPETITION 190–95 (1933). But Mrs. Robinson's conclusion is that even imperfect price discrimination is more likely to increase than to reduce output. *Id.* at 200–02.

To complete our discussion of discrimination, let us briefly consider the objections to it. It is commonly said to have undesirable secondary effects on the allocation of resources. Thus, if a change from a single price to price discrimination raises transportation charges to aluminum producers, the increased cost of aluminum will tend to shift demand to substitute products although the actual cost to society of transporting aluminum has not risen. On the other hand, the monopolist has good reasons of self-interest for not carrying discrimination to the point where major substitution effects occur. If a railroad raises its rate to aluminum producers by so much that aluminum users reduce their purchases, there will be less business for the railroad. Our earlier point, then, governs: If the monopolist can discriminate perfectly he will not charge prices that result in turning away any remunerative business. If he cannot discriminate perfectly, discrimination may have undesirable secondary effects.

A monopolist may have difficulty enforcing a finely discriminatory rate structure. Those who purchase at lower rates will have an incentive to resell to those in higher rate brackets. To prevent this kind of arbitrage, the monopolist may be forced into policing activity that is costly and that may run afoul of the long-standing public policy, held by the Supreme Court to be implicit in the Sherman Act,[48] against restraints on alienation. However, these problems would probably not be general in natural monopoly industries, since, as mentioned, the output of such industries typically consists of services that are not readily transferable. Even in the absence of formal measures to prevent arbitrage, then, it would be unlikely to erupt on a very large scale.

Discrimination is also challenged as an unfair method of competition, but we shall see later in this Article that the charge is questionable.[49] In sum, discrimination may be consistent with and even necessary to allocative efficiency. It is also the policy one would expect an unregulated monopolist to adopt voluntarily since it would maximize his profit. By that very token, discrimination aggravates the distributive effects of monopoly; it enables the monopolist to appropriate even more of the consumers' surplus than if he charged a single price. But that does not alter our point that, given discrimination,

[48]Most recently in United States v. Arnold, Schwinn & Co., 388 U.S. 365, 377–78 (1967).

[49]See text accompanying notes 127–29 infra.

the extent to which unregulated natural monopoly leads to allocative inefficiency is uncertain.

The argument, finally, that possession of monopoly profits dulls the incentive to make additional profits—so that a comfortably prosperous firm will seek less assiduously for ways of reducing its costs in order to increase its profits than a lean firm—is plausible but, when one reflects on the actual financial structure of a publicly held corporation, unconvincing. The only individuals in a position to reap monopoly profits are those who own stock at the time that the monopoly is first obtained or first becomes valuable. As soon as it becomes known that a firm has a valuable monopoly, the price of its stock will rise as a means of discounting the anticipated future profits. Subsequent purchasers of the stock will not earn a monopoly return on *their* investment, nor will original owners derive any additional benefit from the firm's monopoly position beyond that reflected in the present value of their stock, until and unless the firm increases its profits. Current owners of a monopolist thus have the same incentive to improve the firm's earnings as the owners of a competitive firm.

B. *Internal Inefficiency*

In discussing the implications of monopoly for efficiency I have heretofore been concerned with how the price system allocates the nation's stock of economic resources among different industries to meet consumer wants at the lowest social cost. Another important, and to the layman a more familiar, kind of efficiency is cost minimization by the firm, which I shall call "internal efficiency."[50] I limit the term to mean the best possible use of a firm's resources within the existing state of technology. Efforts to reduce costs through advancing the state of the art are discussed in the next subpart under "innovation."

In a competitive market, the drive to minimize costs has aspects both of the carrot and of the stick. By reducing costs, the firm can obtain greater profits, either by continuing to sell at the market price or by shading that price and thus increasing its volume of sales. But the benefits are likely to be short-lived as competitors match the cost re-

---

[50]For the distinction between allocative and internal (or, to the economist, "technical" or "X") efficiency see Leibenstein, *supra* note 42; Williamson, *Economies as an Antitrust Defense: The Welfare Tradeoffs,* 58 AM. ECON. REV. 18 (1968).

ductions and adjust price as their own costs fall in order to take maximum advantage of the new cost level. It is concern for survival that provides the strongest incentive to cost reduction by the competitive firm. If it fails to match a rival's cost reduction, possibly if it fails to anticipate a rival's cost reduction, it may find itself fatally disadvantaged.

In the case of a monopolist the carrot is larger but the stick smaller. Cost reduction will enable the monopolist to increase its profits, and with less concern that the effect will be short-lived, since it has no rivals. But concerns for survival ordinarily play no part. The assumptions one makes about a monopolist's corporate objectives are thus quite important here. Certainly a monopolist who is a strict profit maximizer will be powerfully motivated to minimize his costs. It is difficult to argue that his motivation will be significantly less, on balance, than that of the competitive firm. Regrettably, a strong motivation to be efficient does not guarantee efficiency. Firms differ in their ability to minimize cost. Under competition, a firm either learns from its most efficient rival or goes under; either way production ends up at the least-cost level. The situation is more complex under monopoly. On the one hand, few entire industries (defining an industry as all the firms in the country that sell a particular good or service) are natural monopolies. Even the Bell System, which comes close to monopolizing the telephone industry, is a federation of semi-autonomous regional operating companies rather than a monolith. Generally, it is the regional or local market that can accommodate only a single firm. Within an industry, then, there will be a number of firms operating in separate markets and each firm will have a strong incentive to reduce costs. There should be sufficient diversity to produce many useful examples for emulation by the others, much as under competition.

On the other hand, conditions of cost and demand may vary significantly from market to market, and that will complicate efforts to borrow from efficient counterparts. A firm studying the methods employed in another market may have difficulty in determining whether lower costs in the other market stem from external factors or superior methods, and if the latter whether they are applicable to the problems that it faces in its own market. In short, even assuming that monopolists are assiduous profit maximizers in the conventional sense and hence strongly motivated to minimize their costs, one would still be concerned that those monopolists who, despite motivation, lacked great talent for cost minimization might have trouble imitating their more efficient cousins.

If managers of a monopoly firm exploit their opportunities to pursue ends other than immediate profit maximization, additional problems of internal efficiency may arise. Let us suppose that Firm A, a monopolist, is managed by Mr. X, who owns no stock in the corporation and who, because the stock of the corporation is widely dispersed and because all of the directors of A are members of management, controls the firm with minimum regard for the stockholders' interests. In a good year, with profits running to 30 percent of equity capital after taxes, X raises his salary by an amount equal to one-half of the firm's profits. Formally this is a substitution of a cost item (salary) for profits, and increases the firm's costs. Actually it is no such thing; it is a diversion of monopoly profits to X. The firm has not consumed any economic resources unnecessarily, but has simply distributed part of its profits to someone other than the stockholders.

X's action causes a murmur of disapproval among the stockholders, so the next year, rather than skim off some of the firm's monopoly profits in the form of salary, he splendidly refurnishes his office at a cost to the company of $100,000. It is possible that this expenditure, too, represents nothing more than a diversion of monopoly profits to X, but that would be true only if X, had he felt free to take a slice of the firm's profits in money, would have devoted $100,000 of his own money to refurnishing his office. He may have better things to do with $100,000. He may derive less utility from refurnishing his office than he would from refurnishing his home. If so, the translation of monopoly profits into a business expense wasted resources: The economic welfare of society (of which X, of course, is a member) would have been greater if X had been given the $100,000 directly.

Managerial self-indulgence of the kind illustrated in these examples may not be terribly serious from the standpoint of internal efficiency. It is largely (although as the last example shows not entirely) a matter of how monopoly profits are allocated between stockholders and managers, rather than how efficiently the firm is run.[51] More-

[51]It could, however, distort the allocation of managerial talent as between monopoly and nonmonopoly firms. Good managers might gravitate to the former because of the greater rewards available. This might lead to a general bidding up of managerial costs in relation to those of other factors of production.

over, it is not clear that managerial self-indulgence is either particularly widespread among major firms or involves large amounts of money. The growing professionalism and bureaucratization of corporate management should prevent gross excesses in this area. Most important, in a corporation with annual revenues of hundreds of millions of dollars, the amounts diverted by management to its own use (whether directly or in perquisites) above reasonable compensation are not likely to be substantial in relation to the corporation's sales or even profits.

What could be more serious is the subordination of immediate profit maximization to long-term firm and managerial interest in security, prestige, entrenchment, and political power and acceptability. A management not forced to reduce costs to the bone in order to survive is free to take a more strategic attitude toward corporate and personal destiny than one constrained by the market to pursue cost minimization and immediate profit maximization. Such a management may see value in acceding to the demands of labor unions after only nominal resistance in order to enlist union support in Congress or state legislatures behind legislation favorable to the firm's interests. It may decide to spend large sums on public relations in order to generate a favorable climate of opinion that might some day be useful in warding off legislation that the firm opposes or obtaining legislation it favors. It may give favorable pricing treatment to politically powerful purchasers such as the federal government. It may use its own purchases as a way of dispensing patronage to potentially useful allies in the business community. It may locate plants with a view toward maximizing the political support that it can generate in furtherance of its objectives. It may overinnovate in order to impress the public with its progressiveness.[52]

This danger may be termed industrial politicization. Instead of pursuing a single-minded policy of profit maximizing in the short term, the firm recognizes the long-run value of building political support through corporate image and influence building and invests substantial sums in that pursuit. Such policies may require the firm to operate at an inefficient level of expenditure, although that is not a necessary implication. An excessively generous wage settlement with a union may represent simply a distribution of a portion of the firm's monopoly profits to its workers, analogous to the distribution

[52]For some evidence relating to regulated monopolists see note 102 *infra*.

to managers discussed earlier. (A settlement involving an agreement not to lay off unneeded workers might, in contrast, represent a real cost.) Nor would it be sound to regard all corporate efforts to influence the political process as wasteful or improper. If other groups use the political process to advance their economic welfare—as of course they do—business firms cannot reasonably be asked to abstain. One way of building political goodwill, finally, is to forgo monopoly profits, although that might leave some important potential sources of support, such as labor, unappeased.

In the absence of any systematic empirical study one can only guess at the gravity of the problem under discussion. I suspect that monopoly power is not the crucial variable. Competitive firms, after all, do many of the same things through trade associations. A more important variable may be the industry's involvement with government. Although the textile industry is competitive, one would expect a textile manufacturer having government contracts to consider the probable reaction of powerful Congressmen very carefully before relocating a plant or making some other major business move that could have political repercussions, and one dependent on continued government curtailment of imports to weigh carefully the probable reaction of the White House to any attempt to reduce labor costs.

One might be concerned, finally, that a monopolist who lacked the discipline of profit maximization might simply allow costs to drift upward toward his monopoly price, tolerating inefficiency until his profits were deeply eroded. But this assumes that the firm that does not maximize profit has no other maximands. Whether management is seeking to line its own pockets, to build pyramids, or to accumulate political support, failure to exercise close cost control will only impair its objectives. A more plausible hypothesis is that the organizational characteristics of the modern large firm preclude effective cost control except in response to conditions of adversity; but convincing evidence is thus far lacking.[53]

Although we do not know the extent to which internal inefficiency is a serious problem of monopoly, it could be substantially more se-

---

[53]*See* discussion in note 9 *supra*. In speaking of "cost" control in this context, I am, of course, distinguishing between those costs that constitute the managers' expense preferences (*e.g.*, fancy offices), and all other costs. Management will by definition not seek to minimize the former category of costs, but it has every incentive to minimize all other costs; and we earlier saw that managerial expense preferences are very often not real costs at all but simply an indirect form of monopoly profit.

rious than the more familiar problem of monopoly profits. Quite apart from our earlier point that monopoly profits may not deserve a great deal of worry, one should note that to incur an unnecessary expense wastes more of society's resources than jacking up price by the same amount in order to return investors' monopoly profits. By increasing price, the higher costs produce the same restriction of output as if the price had been inflated by an equivalent monopoly profit. Other than possibly restricting output, however, a monopoly profit merely transfers wealth from the buyer to the seller; society's stock of resources is not directly diminished. But money expended to hire more of the factors of production than actually needed to conduct a business diverts resources from more productive activities, and this effect is not only additive to, but could be many times greater than, the social cost in allocative inefficiency.[54]

C. *Failure To Optimize the Rate and Direction of Technological Change*

Although technological progress has been enormously important in increasing the standard of living in advanced countries, we know relatively little about the market environment most conducive to such progress. Formidable difficulties in measuring technological progress and in disentangling multiple causes have made empirical study thus far inconclusive. We are remitted largely to theory.

Innovation exhibits several rather special characteristics. First, it is expensive; the costs of inventive activity, which are frequently substantial, must be incurred before—often long before—any revenues can be realized. Second, innovation is a risky activity for a private firm to undertake; both cost and success are difficult to predict. From these facts it follows that firms are unlikely to innovate unless the payoff from successful innovation is quite large. In addition, the high degree of uncertainty that characterizes inventive activity implies the importance of pursuing a number of diverse approaches toward the desired breakthrough, since any one is quite likely to fail. A third distinctive characteristic of invention is that its essence is knowledge. Once used, knowledge can readily be appropriated by others. The

---

[54]Assuming a relatively inelastic demand, the welfare loss occasioned by a price increase, due to market power, of 20 percent may be completely offset by a reduction in cost of 1 percent. *See* Williamson, *supra* note 50, at 22–23. Conversely, modest cost increases create more serious welfare losses than relatively large price increases arising solely from market power. *See also* Comanor & Leibenstein, *Allocative Efficiency, X-Efficiency and the Measurement of Welfare Losses* (to be published in AM. ECON. REV. PAPERS & PROCEEDINGS (May 1969)).

successful innovator may have difficulty in reaping private benefits equal to the social benefits of his work. If he cannot do so the rate of innovation may be suboptimal.

The foregoing factors define the essential elements of sustained and effective inventive activity by private firms: the resources to enable heavy expenses to be incurred well in advance of any possible payoff; the incentive to incur the costs and the risks of innovation, which in turn depends both on a large payoff if the benefits of the innovation can be appropriated by the inventor and a reasonable prospect that he will in fact be able to appropriate them; and a sufficient diversity of paths to breakthrough. To what extent are these conditions fulfilled in a monopolistic as compared to a competitive environment?

By virtue of enjoying monopoly profits, a monopolist at any given moment may have relatively more resources to devote to inventive activity than a firm whose profits are limited by competition. But possession of resources does not dictate their use for a particular purpose. Moreover, if a competitive firm has reason to anticipate that innovation will yield a substantial profit it should be able to raise the required funds in the capital market. Thus, if the prospects of innovation seem bright, both the monopolist and the competitive firm should be able to finance the necessary R & D, the former because it has, and the latter because it has access to, the necessary resources. This comparison seems a standoff.

At first blush, one might imagine that the competitive firm would have more to gain from successful innovation than a monopolist, and hence a greater incentive to innovate. An innovation that reduces the cost of a product sold under competitive conditions enables the innovator to reduce his price, and if by doing so he can drive out his competitors and obtain a monopoly of the market, he will be able to appropriate as monopoly profit a great deal of the extra value, above cost, that consumers attach to the product. The monopolist, in contrast, is presumably already capturing much of the consumers' surplus available in his market. A reduction in his costs would enable him only to capture some more.[55]

---

[55]I had thought, on a first reading, that this was the argument made by Arrow, *Economic Welfare and the Allocation of Resources for Invention*, in THE RATE AND DIRECTION OF INVENTIVE ACTIVITY: ECONOMIC AND SOCIAL FACTORS 609, 619–22 (Nat'l Bureau Econ. Research 1962). While the argument still seems to me an interesting one, I am now convinced that it is not the argument presented by Arrow. If I understand it correctly,

This point requires qualification in two important respects. First, it is primarily applicable to innovations whose only consequence is to reduce the cost of the monopolist's existing product. A monopolist has an incentive equal to a competitive firm's so far as inventions applicable to markets not presently monopolized by him are concerned. And even within his monopolized markets he has a very strong incentive to product innovation; for if he develops a better product his demand curve may shift sharply to the right—that is, consumers may attach much greater value to what he produces than previously. If so he will be able to appropriate a good deal more consumers' surplus than before, much as a competitive firm could. Thus, before A. T. & T. laid the first undersea telephone cable in 1956, its international telephone service was not greatly in demand because the quality of radiotelephone service was poor and the capacity was limited. Innovation created a service that was much more valuable to the consumer and that in consequence began immediately to make substantial inroads into substitute services such as telegraphy.[56]

Second, while the potential payoff from cost-reducing if not from product-improving innovations may be greater for the competitive firm than for the monopolist, the likelihood that the competitive firm

---

his argument is that an inventor of a process that reduced the cost of a product produced under competitive conditions could demand a royalty equal to a fraction less than the difference between the industry's former costs of production and its new, lower costs and that this royalty would exceed the additional profit that a monopolist of the same market would obtain from the same innovation. The reason why the monopolist's gain from innovation is smaller, however, is that the monopolist's output is deemed, by the principle that monopolists restrict output, to be smaller than that of the competitive industry. The same reduction in unit cost, applied to a smaller output, yields a smaller gain from innovation. Therefore, a monopolist will devote fewer resources to innovation than a competitive firm. But this is no more than a special case of the general proposition that a monopolized industry tends to use fewer resources— whether labor, capital, managerial, scientific, or whatever—than an equivalent industry that is competitive; in restricting output, the monopolist reduces his inputs. The implications of this familiar characteristic of monopoly for technological progress are unclear. If output is reduced in one industry because it is monopolized, it will be expanded in others as consumers shift their demand; if fewer resources are invested in innovation in one industry because it is monopolized, if output is reduced, and if therefore the gains from innovation are also reduced, one would expect more resources to be devoted to innovation in other industries, where output is now greater and the gains from innovation correspondingly increased. The overall level of inventive activity should not be greatly affected. This point is developed in a forthcoming article by Harold Demsetz in the *Journal of Law and Economics*.

[56]*See Hearings on Merger of International Telegraph Carriers Before Senate Comm. on Interstate and Foreign Commerce, 86th Cong., 1st Sess. 29–31 (1959).*

can appropriate all or most of the potential gain is often less. Whatever gains accrue from a cost reduction in a monopoly market are securely the monopolist's. He has no rivals to cancel the gains by promptly imitating the innovation and adjusting price accordingly. The extent to which a competitive firm can appropriate the fruits of its inventive activity depends on whether and how long it can keep the innovation secret, how complete the protection obtainable under the patent laws is, and, failing either of these protections, how valuable a headstart over rivals proves to be. Secrecy is an uncertain protection and in many instances out of the question. Patent "monopolies" cannot be equated with economic monopolies; not only is it frequently feasible to "invent around" a patent but patent rights may be costly to defend. And a headstart may or may not be a significant protection against prompt imitation by rivals. In sum, the competitive firm may have somewhat more dramatic prospects than the monopolist from a successful cost-reducing innovation, but it also has less assurance of realizing them.

The tradeoff becomes even more complex when we recall that a monopolist can subordinate short-term to long-term profit goals. Because of the enormous prestige of science and technology in this society—our almost religious veneration for material progress—a management not constrained by competition to minimize costs in the short run may attach high (perhaps excessive) importance to rapid and productive innovation as a matter of self-esteem and corporate image. The example of the Bell Telephone Laboratories, perhaps the foremost privately owned industrial laboratory in the world, indicates the dividends in public goodwill that a monopolist can obtain by supporting a substantial R & D effort. It should also be noted that a cost reduction permits a monopolist to reduce price without sacrificing profits. Indeed, profit maximization *requires* that the monopolist reduce his price when his costs decline, albeit not by the full amount of the cost reduction.[57] Consumers who see the price of a service falling (or the quality of the service improving) are unlikely to complain vociferously about monopoly prices and profits. That fact should make innovating highly attractive to a firm concerned with the long-run political viability of its monopoly.

[57]This is best illustrated graphically: Under cost condition MC, the profit-maximizing monopolist will sell at price p, the price at which marginal revenue equals marginal cost. Suppose costs decline to MC'. If the monopolist remains at price p, his monopoly profit is the area $ApCD$; if he reduces price to p', where his marginal rev-

This conclusion may seem to contradict J. R. Hicks' well-known dictum, "The best of all monopoly profits is a quiet life."[58] A pure *ipse dixit* when offered, the remark has never been substantiated; I earlier expressed my doubt whether the image of the sated monopolist corresponds to reality.[59] In any event, one would suppose that a monopolist who wanted to enjoy a "quiet life" *would* innovate, sacrificing some immediate profits for long-run security against technological displacement. No natural monopoly can safely be assumed by owners or managers to be ordained to last forever, impervious to changes in technology and consumer taste. The monopolist must always reckon with the possibility of being supplanted as a result of technological change. It behooves him to anticipate such change through an active R & D program. And conducted on a substantial scale by a substantial firm, R & D is hardly so adventurous or unpredictable as to require a gambler's temperament. There is a good correlation between increased R & D expenditures and enhanced profitability,[60] and no reason, therefore, why a moderately cautious firm should be deterred from an adequate innovative effort.

enue is equal to his new marginal cost, *MC'*, then his monopoly profit is the area *Ep'BD*. It can be demonstrated mathematically that this area is always larger than *ApCD*. However, if the demand curve is shifting to the right at the same time costs are decreasing, the new profit-maximizing price may be higher than the old.

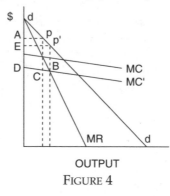

OUTPUT

FIGURE 4

[58]*Annual Survey of Economic Theory: The Theory of Monopoly*, 3 ECONOMETRICA, 1, 8 (1935), *reprinted in* READINGS IN PRICE THEORY 361, 369 (Am. Econ. Ass'n 1952).
[59]*See* text between notes 49 and 50 *supra*.
[60]*See* E. MANSFIELD, THE ECONOMICS OF TECHNOLOGICAL CHANGE 65–67, 106 (1968); E. MANSFIELD, INDUSTRIAL RESEARCH AND TECHNOLOGICAL INNOVATION—AN ECONOMETRIC ANALYSIS 199–201, 203–04 (1968).

On the other hand, concern for survival provides a greater incentive to rapid innovation for the competitive than for the monopoly firm. A firm that fails to anticipate a competitor's innovation may be destroyed, and although some monopolists have suffered grievously from the innovations of potential competitors (such as Western Union vis-à-vis the telephone companies) one would expect a monopolist to feel less concern about being preempted. In this respect, the motivation to innovate is stronger under competition than under monopoly.[61]

How do the diverse incentives of competitors and of monopolists net out? What market structure provides the greatest overall incentive to innovate? One can only guess at the answer. Before leaving the subject of incentives. I should mention the prevalent notion that a monopolist will not introduce an innovation as early as would a competitive firm for fear of being unable to recover its existing investment. It is true that a monopolist will not introduce a new process unless the total cost of the new is less than the marginal cost of the old. These are the respective current costs of the processes and that is the only comparison relevant in determining a firm's conduct; sunk costs are bygones. But the same principle governs the introduction of innovations in a competitive setting. A firm with a new process will not introduce it unless its total cost is below the marginal cost of competitors using the old. Unless that condition is fulfilled the new process is not competitive, since as we saw in our railroad example a firm in pricing will ignore sunk costs if necessary to repel a new entrant.[62] Hence one would expect the monopolist and the competitive firm to have identical incentives with respect to the timing of the introduction of new processes.

[61]*See* Scherer, *Research and Development Resource Allocation Under Rivalry*, 81 Q.J. ECON, 359 (1967).

[62]*See* text accompanying notes 45–46 *supra*; Fellner, *The Influence of Market Structure on Technological Progress*, 65 Q.J. ECON. 556, 572–73 (1951), *reprinted in* READING IN INDUSTRIAL ORGANIZATION AND PUBLIC POLICY 277, 292–93 (Am. Econ. Ass'n 1958). A well-known empirical study of the electric-lamp industry is sometimes cited as supporting the proposition that a monopolistic firm will lack incentive to develop new products or processes when it is heavily committed to the old. The study indeed states: "The incentives of General Electric have not been so strong, however, for the rapid development of new light sources for general illumination, which would jeopardize its vested interest in the older incandescent lamp." A. BRIGHT, THE ELECTRIC-LAMP INDUSTRY: TECHNOLOGICAL CHANGE AND ECONOMIC DEVELOPMENT FROM 1800 to 1947, at 455 (1949). This conclusion is not well supported by the study, however, or by other studies of the industry. *See* pages referenced in *id*. at 456; J. JEWKES, D. SAWERS & R. STILLERMAN, THE SOURCES OF INVENTION 298–301 (1958).

More troublesome than any supposed lack of incentive is the possible lack of diversity of approaches to technological breakthrough under monopoly. The process of research and development is to a significant extent one of trial and error. There is advantage, therefore, in the simultaneous pursuit of a variety of approaches to the desired end. Diversity may be difficult to achieve within a single firm due to the homogeneity of its personnel and the standardization of its procedures. Several firms quite different in organization and interests may achieve in the aggregate a more rapid rate of innovation than a single firm that spends the same amount on R & D as the several firms together.

While this is a forceful point, and is corroborated by what empirical studies we have,[63] it does not necessarily imply that innovation in an industry having a monopolistic structure will be suboptimal. As mentioned earlier, it is rare that an entire industry is a natural monopoly. A series of local or regional monopolists engaged in furnishing the same service should provide, therefore, some diversity of approach. Natural monopoly, moreover, is generally a phenomenon of distribution; manufacturers of the equipment used by the natural monopolist are an additional and very important source of diversity in inventive activity. The communications industry is atypical in the foregoing respects. Most of the regional or local monopolists at the distribution level are part of the Bell System, which also controls the major manufacturer of communications equipment, Western Electric. Even so, there is considerable diversity in the relevant R & D, since the concepts, components, and systems of modern communications are quite similar to those of the highly dynamic electronics, computer, and aerospace industries. This example illustrates the important principle that the relevant market in which to appraise the diversity of innovative approaches is generally broader than the usual product or service market. Indeed, the more far-reaching the innovation, the more likely that it emerged in quite a different industry from the one in which it was first exploited commercially. Nylon was invented by the chemical, not the textile, industry. The transistor was invented by the telephone industry, not the radio or television or computer industries. The synchronous communications satellite was invented by the aerospace rather than by the communi-

---

[63]See, e.g., J. JEWKES, D. SAWERS & R. STILLERMAN, supra note 62, at 222, 246–47; Devons, The Aircraft Industry, in 2 THE STRUCTURE OF BRITISH INDUSTRY 45 (D. Burn ed. 1958).

cations industry.[64] The fact that an industry is a monopoly does not mean that only one firm is pursuing R & D in its technology.[65]

The importance of external sources reinforces our earlier suggestion that a monopolist will feel pressure to innovate in order to forestall the emergence of competitors. An electronics firm engaged in research into the nature of electromagnetic radiation may discover a technique of communications that enables it to supplant a communications carrier in one of its markets. The carriers have every interest in anticipating such a development. The railroad industry would have benefited greatly from developing the truck and introducing trucking as an extension, rather than a competitor, of rail transportation.

A mainly theoretical analysis has yielded little support for the view that monopolists are on balance less likely to innovate than more competitive enterprises.[66] The picture is much the same when we turn to the empirical literature. The evidence to date yields no clear relationship between technological progressiveness and any particular kind of market structure.[67] Very possibly other factors, such as absolute corporate size or the pattern of research outside of the corporate sector, are much more important to technological progress than the degree of competition. One should note, however,

[64]This is a good example of the importance of diversity, even without competition. Both U.S. domestic long-haul communications and U.S. international satellite communications are monopolies, but of different companies—A.T.&T. and Comsat. A.T.&T. did not believe that synchronous satellites were feasible; Comsat did, and its judgment has been vindicated.

[65]The importance of external sources is stressed by E. MANSFIELD, THE ECONOMICS OF TECHNOLOGICAL CHANGE 110–12 (1968).

[66]Since, as noted earlier, the achievement of the least-cost level by monopolists may be more difficult than by competitive firms, *see* text following note 50 *supra*, it is quite possible that the diffusion of an innovation throughout an industry composed of a series of regional or local monopolists will be slower than in a competitive industry. That is not to say, however, that the state of the art is advanced less rapidly under monopoly, but only that it may take longer for all firms in a noncompetitive industry to take advantage of the inventive efforts of their most progressive counterparts or suppliers, as of other cost-saving opportunities.

[67]This is the conclusion of a good recent survey of the empirical studies. E. MANSFIELD, *supra* note 65, at 215–17. To similar effect see D. HAMBERG, R&D: ESSAYS ON THE ECONOMICS OF RESEARCH AND DEVELOPMENT 68 (1966); R. NELSON, M. PECK & E. KALACHEK, TECHNOLOGY, ECONOMIC GROWTH AND PUBLIC POLICY 66–72 (1967); Brozen, *R&D Differences Among Industries,* in ECONOMICS OF RESEARCH AND DEVELOPMENT 83 (R. Tybout ed. 1965); Scherer, Comment in *id.* at 129. Most of the empirical studies have been comparisons of various degrees of oligopoly; there have been few studies of innovation by monopolists. Peck, *Inventions in the Postwar American Aluminum Industry,* in THE RATE AND DIRECTION OF INVENTIVE ACTIVITY: ECONOMIC AND SOCIAL FACTORS 279,

that if monopolistic industries *are* less progressive than competitive industries, the consequences could be quite serious. Technological change, which has created many valuable new products and often reduced the costs of existing products by entire orders of magnitude, is probably more important to the economic welfare of society than static efficiency, either allocative or internal.[68]

D. *Arbitrary Refusals To Serve, Inferior Goods and Service, and Unresponsiveness to Consumer Wants*

One of the common beliefs about monopolists is that they are unresponsive to the consumer's desires because he has no choice—that they decline on capricious grounds to serve particular customers, are rude, and sell shoddy goods and provide poor service. The charge is seriously overstated, although it has a core of truth.

The argument that a monopolist is likely to be arrogant or capricious in his treatment of the consumer is supported by analogy to the treatment that minor governmental functionaries occasionally mete out to the hapless citizen. The charge makes more sense in the latter than in the former case. A minor functionary, protected in his job by political influence or civil service rules, may have nothing to gain from adopting a cooperative and polite attitude toward the members of the public with whom he deals, and he may derive psychological satisfaction from abusing them. A monopolist has a different set of incentives. The management of the Bell System or of the Pacific Gas & Electric Company can derive little psychic satisfaction from alienating customers and can fire any employees who do. If a monopolist arbitrarily refuses service to an individual, it not only gratuitously impairs public goodwill, but loses the profits that it would have obtained by serving him. A refusal to deal, therefore, is likely to reflect a yielding to powerful forces (such as intense and widespread racial

---

294 (Nat'l Bureau Econ. Research 1962), attributes the greater rate of invention in the aluminum industry after World War II to the replacement of Alcoa's monopoly by a three-firm oligopoly. He notes that Reynolds and Kaiser, although together only about the size of Alcoa, were both responsible for as many inventions; and he reasons that Alcoa would not have been thrice as inventive had it been twice as large. Perhaps not, but I have difficulty understanding the basis of the conjecture. Kendrick, in a study of productivity growth in the American economy, found that the regulated industries have done better than the national average. Productivity Trends in the U.S. Private Economy and in the Public Utilities, 1948–1966, Apr. 24, 1968 (unpublished). This is far from conclusive, since these industries may have been the passive beneficiaries of the inventive efforts of others.

[68]*See* R. NELSON, M. PECK & E. KALACHEK, *supra* note 67, at 16–18; E. MANSFIELD, *supra* note 65, at 4–5; *cf.* J. SCHUMPETER, CAPITALISM, SOCIALISM AND DEMOCRACY 83 (1942).

prejudice in the community) that would be equally effective against competitive firms.

The notion that a monopolist will produce a less durable good than a competitive firm or render poorer service or otherwise degrade the quality of what he sells is true only in this limited sense: Since reduced quality usually means reduced cost, a firm that acquires a monopoly of a good or service formerly sold in competition may be able to make a monopoly profit by holding price constant and reducing quality as well as by holding quality constant and increasing price. That is not to say, however, that the monopolist is indifferent to quality. The decision whether to degrade quality or increase price will be guided by the cost of different levels of quality and the value that the consumer attaches to them. If consumers in the aggregate will pay $1,000 for widgets that cost $600 to produce and $1,100 for a better grade that costs the monopolist $680, he will produce the better grade. If they will pay only $1,079, indicating an unwillingness to shoulder the extra expense of the better product, the monopolist will be guided by that preference.[69]

Far from being indifferent to quality, then, the monopolist has a strong incentive to determine consumers' reactions to various quality-price combinations. Nor is it cogent to argue that in the absence of competitive choice consumers' wants are difficult to gauge accurately. There is nothing to prevent a monopolist from probing them through the same devices used by competitive firms to develop new markets—market research, advertising, sales promotions, and test marketing. He has every incentive to be ingenious in anticipating and responding to consumers' wants.

E. *Ruinous or Wasteful Competition*

Thus far I have been discussing the equilibrium state of a natural monopoly market or industry: a single firm supplying the market's entire demand. Sometimes, however, several firms may find themselves in such a market. A market that once supported several firms, each operating at efficient scale, may, by reason of imperfectly anticipated technological change, become a natural monopoly before the firms (minus one) have made graceful exits. If these firms compete vigorously, competition will be short-lived. The most efficient firm will survive and the others fail or be acquired by it. If, however, by outright collusion or by adopting a policy of "live and let live" the

<hr>

[69]*See* Stigler, *A Theory of Oligopoly*, 72 J. Pol. Econ. 44, 61 (1964), *reprinted in* G. Stigler, The Organization of Industry 39, 62 (1968).

firms in a natural monopoly market refrain from vigorous—and literally destructive—competition, production will persist at an inefficient scale, since by definition the most efficient way of supplying the market's entire demand is by one firm.

The possibility that more than one firm will find itself selling in a natural monopoly market is not, however, a substantial basis of concern about performance under natural monopoly. The situation is inherently unstable. Either there will be a brief flurry of fierce competition that leaves one firm in clear command of the field, forcing the others to merge with it or to fail, or—even more likely, one would think—there will be mergers without a period of fierce competition. The firms will realize that they can do much better by merging, operating at an efficient scale, and reaping monopoly profits than by either (1) competing to the death or (2) continuing multi-firm production at higher costs and lower profits than if they were consolidated.

If this reasoning is correct, there is not much substance to the conventional view, upon which regulation of the transportation industries is largely founded,[70] that in an industry where the economies of scale are substantial unregulated competition will cause chronic excess capacity leading to sustained and ruinous price wars. On the contrary, one would expect the firms in such an industry to consolidate their facilities and retire such capacity as was excess. So suggesting, I do not deny that railroads were overbuilt in the 19th century (partly as a result of governmental subsidy)[71] or that there were rate wars. But apparently the wars were relatively few and sporadic,[72] and the industry might have shaken down through consolidations had not the Supreme Court held railroad consolidations illegal per se under the Sherman Act.[73] A costly transition may have

[70]See note 2 supra and sources cited therein.

[71]See, e.g., M. FAINSOD, L. GORDON & J. PALAMOUNTAIN, GOVERNMENT AND THE AMERICAN ECONOMY 115–16 (3d ed. 1959).

[72]E. TROXEL, ECONOMICS OF TRANSPORT 428–32, 656, 726 (1955). Moreover, most of the rate wars apparently were not caused by excess capacity. See P. MACAVOY, THE ECONOMIC EFFECTS OF REGULATION: THE TRUNK-LINE RAILROAD CARTELS AND THE INTERSTATE COMMERCE COMMISSION BEFORE 1900, at 195 n.3 (1965). For trenchant criticisms of the ruinous-competition theory see C. KAYSEN & D. TURNER, ANTITRUST POLICY 196 (1959); Boies, Experiment in Mercantilism: Minimum Rate Regulation by the Interstate Commerce Commission, 68 COLUM. L. REV. 599, 660–63 (1968); Reynolds, Cutthroat Competition, 30 AM. ECON. REV. 736 (1940).

[73]See United States v. Southern Pac. Co., 259 U.S. 214 (1922); United States v. Union Pac. Ry. Co., 226 U.S. 61 (1912); Northern Sec. Co. v. United States, 193 U.S. 197, 331 (1904); additional cases cited in M. CONANT, RAILROAD MERGERS AND ABANDONMENTS

been inevitable. What is difficult to accept is that the situation would not eventually have corrected itself without government intervention.

As just implied, however, a possible problem in relying on natural market forces to match the number of firms in a market to the market's cost conditions is the antitrust laws. If as the Supreme Court has intimated economies of scale will not excuse a merger that may substantially lessen competition,[74] sellers in a natural monopoly market cannot lawfully merge until the brink of failure is reached. This impediment to efficiency could be eliminated by recognizing natural monopoly as a defense in a merger proceeding. Such a defense would complicate merger litigation, perhaps seriously, but only in a few cases. That may be a risk worth taking to avoid the serious and protracted inefficiencies that could result if the sellers in a natural monopoly market (who should be few enough to effectuate a policy of avoiding price competition without detectable collusion) decide not to embark on the risky course of determining through price competition who shall survive. On the other hand, it may not be strictly necessary to recognize a formal defense. One can probably rely on the Department of Justice in the exercise of its enforcement discretion not to proceed in such a case, although the Department has not been explicit on the point.[75]

F. *Unfair Competition*

One of the oldest complaints against monopoly is that a monopolist will annex a competitive market by using the monopoly profits from his other markets to subsidize a price that his competitors cannot meet because it is below cost. Recent studies, however, have cast doubt on whether "predatory price discrimination" is much of a danger.[76] Certainly if profit maximization is assumed to be the mo-

---

47–48 (1964). *See also* Louisville & N.R.R. v. Kentucky, 161 U.S. 677 (1896); Pearsall v. Great Northern Ry., 161 U.S. 646 (1896), where state statutes prohibiting railroad consolidations were sustained.

[74]*See* FTC v. Procter & Gamble Co., 386 U.S. 568, 580 (1967) (dictum); Brown Shoe Co. v. United States, 370 U.S. 294, 344 (1962) (dictum).

[75]The Department has publicly indicated that only in "exceptional circumstances" will it accept economies as a justification for a merger. Department of Justice Merger Guidelines, I TRADE REG. REP. ¶ 4430, at 6684–85 (1968).

[76]*See* McGee, *Predatory Price Cutting: The Standard Oil (N.J.) Case,* 1 J. LAW & ECON. 137 (1958); Telser, *Cutthroat Competition and the Long Purse,* 9 J. LAW & ECON. 259, 267 (1966); Turner, *Conglomerate Mergers and Section 7 of the Clayton Act,* 78 HARV. L. REV. 1313, 1339–52 (1965).

nopolist's strategy, predatory pricing is a tactic of questionable advantage in most cases. It requires the monopolist to forgo present profits in the hope that he will be able to charge a monopoly price in the competitive market (once he has monopolized it) that will more than recoup his earlier losses. But charging a monopoly price in a market that by definition has a competitive structure will attract new entrants, and the process of predation will have to be repeated indefinitely, with all the losses that the process entails. A possible exception is where entry into the market is difficult. Suppose that, due to economies of scale, a particular market will accommodate only three firms of efficient size. If one of those firms drives out the others, it may be able to raise its price somewhat without attracting entry by a new firm, because of the difficulty involved in large-scale entry. On the other hand, a structural characteristic such as economies of scale that makes entry into a market difficult may also affect the vigor of competition among the existing firms in the market. The three firms in our example might tacitly collude to keep their price as high as was possible without inducing new entry. If so, none of them could anticipate a higher profit rate by driving out the others. Indeed, a firm whose monopoly is not justified by economies of scale may be more vulnerable to the inroads of a new entrant than a cartel of smaller firms, for the single firm may encounter *dis*economies of scale.[77] Furthermore, the very factors that create barriers to new entry may retard the exit of existing firms and make the process of monopolization by below-cost selling protracted and hence exceedingly expensive, while postponing the time at which recoupment can begin. And when that time comes the monopolist may find that the barriers to entry on which it relied to enable it to charge a monopoly price without inducing prompt new entry have disappeared as the result of technological change. Such considerations would appear to make predatory price cutting a dubious tactic in virtually all circumstances.

If the monopolist believes that a monopoly of the competitive market, once achieved, will remain durable without resort to predatory tactics, his wisest course is to buy out the firms in the competitive market. He can well afford to pay the owners something more than the value of the firms as competitive enterprises—to wit, a share of

[77]*See* Williamson, *Hierarchical Control and Optimum Firm Size*, 75 J. POL. ECON. 123 (1967).

the monopoly profits that he will enjoy when the market is monopolized (appropriately discounted to reflect the fact that they are prospective profits only). The owners will be eager to sell at a premium above the value of their enterprises in the existing competitive setting. What is striking about putting a monopoly together by the merger route—the classical[78] as well as the sensible way of monopolizing—is that it does not require that the monopolizer have a monopoly in some other market. All he need do is convince the sellers in the market that they will be better off if they eliminate competition by merging, and divide the resulting monopoly profits.

One might object that monopolization by merger would involve blatant violation of the antitrust laws, whereas monopolization by below-cost pricing, although equally an antitrust violation,[79] is harder to prove. A merger cannot be fudged; cost questions can. Hence, the very fact that we have a strict law against monopolization by merger may create an inducement to engage in predatory price discrimination that would not otherwise exist. However, the extent to which predatory pricing is possible with impunity is easily exaggerated. A course of pricing that led to an actual monopoly would surely provoke a searching investigation, laying the monopolist open to criminal and heavy civil penalties, including dissolution, as well as to treble-damage actions by his victims. The most recent decision of the Supreme Court in this area[80] has made the law exceedingly severe, possibly too severe. We may now have a set of sanctions that deters not only predatory conduct but some perfectly fair competition as well.

One could argue that the implicit threat of predatory conduct, even if never implemented or implemented so sporadically as to escape detection, should be enough to keep competitors in line and give the firm that monopolizes other markets considerable market power in the competitive market, although not a complete monopoly. If the previous analysis is correct, however, the threat would lack credibility. The competitive firms would know that a ra-

---

[78]See McGee, *supra* note 76; *Investigation of the Telephone Industry in the United States,* H. Doc. No. 340, 76th Cong., 1st Sess. 139–43 (1939).

[79]See Sherman Antitrust Act § 2, 15 U.S.C. § 2 (1964); Clayton Act § 2(a), *as amended,* 15 U.S.C. § 13(a) (1964); Robinson-Patman Antidiscrimination Act § 3, 15 U.S.C. § 13a (1964); Moore v. Mead's Fine Bread Co., 348 U.S. 115 (1954).

[80]Utah Pie Co. v. Continental Baking Co., 386 U.S. 685 (1967).

tional monopolist would not pursue predation seriously. Why should their conduct be affected by a bluff?

Thus far, we have assumed that the monopolist is a strict profit maximizer. If not, he has unexploited monopoly power that he could use to support below-cost selling in competitive markets without impairing his chosen return. But a firm that chooses not to maximize profits is presumably maximizing some other preference that it would have to forgo in order to engage in predatory price cutting (unless the firm is completely passive, which hardly seems compatible with aggression on any front). A significant exception would be a firm seeking to maximize sales or growth.[81] However, of all the ways to build sales, one would imagine predatory price discrimination to be among the least attractive to a monopolist able and inclined (as the sales-maximization hypothesis assumes) to subordinate short-run profit maximization to more strategic goals of corporate and personal gain. Selling below cost is bound to be unpopular, to say the least, among the firms inhabiting the market; it can only draw attention to the monopolist's size and power; and, to repeat, it is both a civil and (if the requisite intent is proved) a criminal violation of the antitrust laws.

At all events, it is striking how few substantiated incidents of predatory pricing have turned up in the annals of American business.[82] With the empirical and theoretical foundations of the fear of predatory price discrimination so thin, and given that we already have strict laws on the books forbidding the practice, it hardly seems to warrant additional regulation.

Another weapon of a monopolist bent on aggrandizement, besides monopoly profits, is buying power. If a monopolist is also a monopsonist (the sole consumer of a product), and if he can establish his own supply facilities, then he is in a position to monopolize the supply market. But it is unclear why he would want a monopoly of supply, when by hypothesis the only customer who could be exploited by such a monopoly would be himself. A wiser tactic for him would be to use his buying power to drive highly favorable terms with the existing suppliers, to ensure, in other words, that he is not exploited.

[81]See text accompanying note 14 supra.

[82]For a review of the evidence see Telser, supra note 76, at 268–70. To be sure, difficulty of detection may have something to do with this. Moreover, before there was settled law against monopolization by merger, firms could be expected to follow that, the less costly, route. See text accompanying note 78 supra.

In some cases, indeed, the monopsonist may be able to obtain inputs below the competitive price. This would happen if the monopsony arose after the suppliers had committed resources to the market that were not readily transferable to other uses. It is possible to demonstrate that a monopsony price, the obverse of the monopoly price, is equally undesirable from the standpoint of efficient allocation. But it does not follow that monopsony pricing is a general problem of monopoly. A local electrical company is a monopolist, but it competes with many other firms both inside and outside the electric-utility industry in the purchase of its supplies. In general, monopoly does not confer monopsony power, and monopsony power may exist independently of monopoly. They are separate problems.

Exploitation of buying power and predatory price discrimination are only two examples of a wide variety of unfair business practices commonly associated with monopoly. Examples of others are vertical integration, patent abuses, tying arrangements, and refusals to deal with potential competitors. Such practices have frequently cropped up in the regulated industries. Examples are the railroads' refusal to carry piggyback vans tendered by motor carriers at the same rates as those tendered by ordinary shippers and the telephone carriers' refusal to permit the attachment to their lines of terminal or interconnection equipment not supplied by them.[83] But none of these practices is uniquely associated with monopolists, and all are within the conventional scope of general antitrust and trade-regulation law.[84]

G. *The Political Dimension of the Monopoly Problem*

Opposition to monopoly is frequently premised on political grounds. Private economic power, epitomized by the monopolist, is thought to endanger democratic processes. Basically, however, the objection is to large firms rather than to monopolists as such. General Dynamics has more power in any sense relevant to the political process than the independent telephone company that serves Rochester, New York, but the latter is a monopolist and the former is not.

---

[83]Both restrictions were recently voided. *See* American Trucking Ass'ns v. Atchison, T. & S.F. Ry., 387 U.S. 397 (1967); Use of the Carterfone Device, 13 F.C.C.2d 420, *on reconsideration*, 14 F.C.C.2d 571 (1968).

[84]*See* Clayton Act §§ 2, 3, 7, 8, *as amended*, 15 U.S.C. §§ 13, 14, 18, 19 (1964); Federal Trade Commission Act § 5, *as amended*, 15 U.S.C. § 45 (1964); Sherman Antitrust Act §§ 1–8, *as amended*, 15 U.S.C. §§ 1–7 (1964).

Scale—the number of workers, managers, shareholders, suppliers, distributors, creditors, and other dependents or potential allies that a firm has—would appear to be a far more important determinant of the firm's political weight than whether it enjoys a monopoly, that is, whether its stockholders (and perhaps managers) receive unjustified returns or its retained earnings are abnormal. The Bell System is the classic instance of a firm that both is a monopolist and is so large in absolute size[85] as to raise the question whether it may not enjoy undue influence in legislative and other political arenas. But one imagines that such political power as it may possess resides in its scale of operations and thus that profit controls would not make much difference.

H. *Managerial Incompetence*

A fair summation of the discussion thus far is that if the management of a firm that enjoys a natural monopoly is reasonably competent, one cannot assert with any confidence that performance is likely to fall greatly short of our economic or social objectives.[86] The traditional economic objection to monopoly—that it leads to suboptimal output of the monopolized product—has a core of validity as applied to the natural monopolist, but there are, as we saw, a good many reasons for questioning whether the allocative effects of unregulated natural monopoly are in fact likely to be serious. In addition, the management of such a monopoly will have strong incentives to press cost reduction and to innovate. And contrary to popular myth a monopolist is not likely to abuse the public, project its monopoly into competitive markets, or enjoy disproportionate political power. The "stick" of competition, as well as the diversity of approach that the existence of competitors would assure, will be lacking; but there is no convincing basis for the view that performance will be markedly affected thereby, although internal ineffi-

[85]The Bell System is the largest private corporation in the world, with annual revenues amounting to $13 billion in 1967. FORTUNE, June 15, 1968, at 217.

[86]It is interesting to note that a careful full-length study of Alcoa's prewar monopoly failed to uncover sufficient evidence of suboptimal performance to justify, in the author's view, any recommendation for governmental action. D. WALLACE, MARKET CONTROL IN THE ALUMINUM INDUSTRY 352–53, 365 (1937). A detailed study of United Shoe Machinery Corporation's monopoly found considerable price discrimination but no persuasive indication that the company was less progressive than it would have been under competition. C. KAYSEN, UNITED STATES v. UNITED SHOE MACHINERY CORPORATION: AN ECONOMIC ANALYSIS OF AN ANTI-TRUST CASE 207–08 (1956).

ciency may be something of a problem. Nor are the distributive effects of natural monopoly profits demonstrably a cause for serious practical concern or moral condemnation.

It is always possible, however, that the management of a monopolist will be incompetent—that it will make foolish mistakes harmful both to the consumer and to the stockholder (such as selling above the monopoly price), but not so obviously foolish as to invite a proxy fight. Under competition, managerial incompetence is not a social problem. The firm with persistently inferior management will simply fail. There is no such automatic corrective in the case of the monopolist. Substitute services eventually may make such inroads as to awaken the owners to the existence of a managerial problem, but even then it may be difficult to determine whether poor management or exogenous factors were responsible since there are no exactly comparable firms as there would be under competition. Thus, the steady decline of telegraph service led to charges that the management of the Western Union Telegraph Company was incompetent; the reply was that telegraphy had simply been outdistanced by telephony and that the trend could not have been reversed by the shrewdest of managements.[87]

II. The Theory and Practice of Public Utility Regulation

In the preceding part an attempt was made to identify those areas of performance in which the existence of a state of unregulated natural monopoly might appear to be cause for some concern. In general, fears about that state were found to be exaggerated. Our focus now shifts to the regulatory process. What are the regulatory controls? How effectively do they constrain business behavior? What are the side effects and other social costs of attempting to regulate natural monopoly? If these seem to exceed the social benefits of regulation, how can the development and continued existence of the institution be explained?

A. *The Mechanics of Regulation*

It may be helpful at the outset to describe briefly the basic workings of the regulatory process, a process that is susceptible of generalization despite the many differences in detail and emphasis among

---

[87]*See* text accompanying notes 143–44 *infra*.

the various public utility and common carrier statutes.[88] The heart of the process is the determination of the overall revenue requirements of the regulated firm. A test year (ordinarily the most recent typical year of operations for which complete data are available) is selected and the firm is asked to submit its operating and other expenses for that year. The regulatory commission reviews the submission and may disallow expense items that either were imprudently incurred or are not properly expenses—for example, an excessive depreciation allowance constituting a disguised return to investors. The allowed cost of service includes an allowance for a "fair return" to stockholders and bondholders who have provided the capital used to render the regulated service. That allowance is computed by multiplying the company's rate base—either the depreciated original or the replacement cost of the assets used in rendering the service—by the "fair rate of return," a composite percentage made up of the interest the corporation must pay bondholders and the estimated cost of attracting and holding the necessary equity capital. The firm then files a tariff schedule designed to enable it to just cover its cost of service including the return allowance.[89]

The determination of a company's costs and rate base and the ascertainment of a fair rate of return involve sufficient complications to discourage the most zealous regulatory agency from conducting such proceedings continuously or even frequently. Commonly, several years elapse between proceedings, and in the interim periods the firm's costs may change from those of the test year. If they decline the firm's profits will increase, because the rate schedule fixed in the last proceeding remains unchanged until the next proceeding. Ordinarily, the firm can retain such profits, even though they exceed the fair

[88]For citations to the relevant statutes and judicial and administrative interpretations, and for general description of the workings of the regulatory process, the reader should consult any of the recent casebooks or economics texts in the regulated-industries field. *E.g.*, W. JONES, CASES AND MATERIALS ON REGULATED INDUSTRIES (1967); C. PHILLIPS, THE ECONOMICS OF REGULATION: THEORY AND PRACTICE IN THE TRANSPORTATION AND PUBLIC UTILITY INDUSTRIES (1965); F. WELCH, CASES AND TEXT ON PUBLIC UTILITY REGULATION (rev. ed. 1968).

[89]In some industries, notably trucking, the rate-base—rate-of-return method is not used, and instead the regulated firm is allowed a percentage of its expenses as profit. For a description of the method see Note, *Operating Ratio—A Rate Base for the Transit Industry*, 51 IOWA L. REV. 417 (1966). The larger the firm's expenses, the greater the return to the stockholders, assuming no increase in capital costs. The firm thus has an incentive to incur excessive operating costs, comparable to the incentive of the rate-base regulated firm to incur excessive capital costs, discussed in text accompanying note 98 *infra*.

rate of return previously determined. If costs rise, the firm will seek and usually obtain the agency's permission to file revised tariffs.

Although the regulated firm normally enjoys substantial latitude in choosing a combination of rates for specific services that will just yield its overall revenue requirements, regulatory agencies do have comprehensive power over specific rates. An agency may disallow a rate if it is "unjust" or "unreasonable" or "unjustly discriminatory." If a competitor or customer of the regulated firm complains about a specific rate—that it is unjustly low (in the case of the competitor) or unjustly high (in the case of the customer)—the agency will hold hearings and, proceeding much like a court, decide whether the complaint has merit. If so, it will order the regulated firm to revise its rate structure.

A regulated firm may not initiate, extend, or abandon a service or construct additional facilities without first obtaining a certificate of public convenience and necessity from the commission. A new firm desiring to enter the regulated business is also subject to this requirement. In addition, regulatory agencies often have broad power over a variety of restrictive practices normally covered by the antitrust laws, for example, tying arrangements, service discriminations, and mergers. Frequently the power to prohibit such arrangements is coupled with the power to approve and, by approving, to immunize them from prosecution under the antitrust laws. Regulatory agencies have additional powers (over accounting practices, financing, intercarrier contracts, and so on), but they are mainly ancillary to the powers mentioned above.

With the general picture now in mind, let us look more closely at the specific regulatory controls.

B. *The Effects of Regulatory Controls*

1. *Limiting the overall profits of the regulated firm.*

Because the core of the monopoly problem, as traditionally conceived, is monopoly prices and profits, the determination of the overall revenue requirements that will just cover the test-year costs of the regulated firm is the heart of the regulatory process. Nonetheless, the social utility of this control is questionable. As explained earlier, the case for placing legal limits on monopoly profits, whether on grounds of social justice or of economic efficiency, is not compelling. What is more, it is questionable whether regulatory agencies in fact exercise much effective control over the profits of the regulated firms and, if they do, whether such control has, on balance, good effects on performance.

One reason for questioning the efficacy of regulatory constraints on profit is the intermittent character of the regulatory determination. As mentioned earlier, in the considerable intervals of "regulatory lag" the profits of the regulated firm will pierce the ceiling imposed by the regulatory agency if, as has frequently been the case in the regulated industries in recent years, costs are falling rapidly. Furthermore, the determination of a "fair rate of return" on equity capital presents formidable difficulties. Conceptually there is no problem: It is the cost of attracting and holding the equity capital necessary to provide the regulated service. In deciding what the cost is, however, the parties to the regulatory proceeding and the commission itself are thrown back on very rough comparisons with other firms and other industries. Frequently these comparisons are circular because they are to other regulated firms. When they are not circular, they are misleading because they compare a regulated firm with firms that are not monopolists and that are engaged in dissimilar businesses.[90] Assuming the company is usually given the benefit of the doubt, the return allowance will often conceal some monopoly profits.

A firm forbidden to raise rates or ordered to reduce them may react by reducing the quality of its product or service. Suppose that consumers will pay $12 for a widget that costs $10 to make and $10 for a slightly inferior widget that costs $8.50. The manufacturer is ordered to reduce his rate from $12 to $10; by substituting the inferior widget he can retain a substantial portion of his monopoly profits. In theory the agency can prevent a regulated firm from degrading the quality of its service but there are serious practical difficulties. To illustrate, if the waiting period for telephone installation lengthens, or the number of busy signals increases, or repairs are slower, the consumer may gain virtually nothing from a rate reduction; yet these changes in the level of service, unless gross, are difficult to detect, prove, or rectify.

Finally, there is a good deal of room for concealment of monopoly profits through adroit accounting. Many close questions of judgment

[90]For recent applications of the comparable-earnings standard see, *e.g.*, Permian Basin Area Rate Cases, 390 U.S. 747, 806–08 (1968); American Tel. & Tel. Co., 9 F.C.C.2d 30, 53–88 (1967). For a good discussion of the difficulty of determining fair rate of return see J. BONBRIGHT, PRINCIPLES OF PUBLIC UTILITY RATES 238–83 (1961).

arise in deciding which assets should be included in the rate base; in valuing those assets; in determining depreciation allowances; and in separating costs between regulated and nonregulated services and between different regulatory jurisdictions (some of which may be very lax).[91] Moreover, where services involve joint or common costs a rational allocation is impossible even in theory. How much of the cost of a telephone handset is assignable to local and how much to interstate telephone service? There is no right answer. It is fair to assume that most doubtful cases are resolved in the company's favor, simply because a regulatory agency is naturally reluctant to displace corporate business judgments unless it seems reasonably clear that management is wrong. The result may be that substantial monopoly profits are obtained that never show up in the profit column of the ledger.

One should note that the foregoing factors are additive and, together, can easily emasculate the profit ceiling. To illustrate, suppose that in the test year the true depreciated original cost of public utility X's assets is $100,000, the true cost of capital 5 percent, the proper depreciation rate 10 percent, and the true operating expenses (defined as all costs other than capital and depreciation) $30,000. On these assumptions, X's annual revenue requirements are $45,000. Suppose, however, that the regulatory agency, uncertain how to compute the capital cost and inclined to resolve doubts in favor of the company, in fact allows X 7.5 percent as a return allowance. Assume further that by exploiting the accounting vagaries associated with rate-base valuation X is able to inflate the rate base by 10 percent, and by judicious allocations of plant between regulated and nonregulated activities and between strict and lax jurisdictions is able to add another 10 percent to the rate base. As a result the allowed rate of return of 7.5 percent and the depreciation allowance of 10 percent are applied to $120,000, not $100,000. Suppose, moreover, that X is able to inflate its operating expenses by 10 percent, and suppose, finally, that at any particular mo-

[91]The literature on valuation problems is voluminous: a perusal of J. BAUER & N. GOLD, PUBLIC UTILITY VALUATION FOR PURPOSES OF RATE CONTROL (1934), and of J. BONBRIGHT, THE VALUATION OF PROPERTY (1937), will give some idea of the magnitude of the problem. On the question of allocating costs between regulated and nonregulated services see, *e.g.*, FPC v. United Gas Pipe Line Co., 386 U.S. 237 (1967), and between different regulatory jurisdictions see, *e.g.*, R. GABEL, DEVELOPMENT OF SEPARATIONS PRINCIPLES IN THE TELEPHONE INDUSTRY (1967). The matter is still further complicated by the fact that the accounting concept of profits differs from the economic concept and may exclude substantial monopoly profits. *See* Bain, *The Profit Rate as a Measure of Monopoly Power*, 55 Q.J. ECON. 271 (1941).

ment in time its actual operating expenses are 5 percent less than its test-year expenses due to the combined effect of regulatory lag and either lower costs or degraded service. A little arithmetic indicates that X's true rate of return is not 5 percent, but 15.5 percent. And that rate is a composite of interest to the bondholders and return to stockholders. If we assume that the capital structure of the company is composed 50 percent of bonds and 50 percent of equity and that the interest rate is 4 percent, the return on stockholders' equity is 27 percent, even though the true cost of equity capital to the firm is only 6 percent.

This is doubtless an extreme example. The standard error in profit regulation is probably less than 450 percent. What is clear, however, is that relatively moderate errors, of the kind that regulatory agencies can scarcely avoid committing given the intractable problems involved in the computation of revenue requirements, can render profit regulation quite ineffectual; for while I do not believe that in fact public utilities are permitted to earn 27 percent for their stockholders, neither do I believe that many unregulated utilities would fix prices that returned them such profits. In all likelihood, either demand conditions would not warrant such high prices, or fear of inducing entry would lead the firm to charge somewhat lower prices. It is thus plausible to argue that profit regulation may have little actual effect on monopoly prices and profits.[92]

Some readers may react by thinking, "Surely regulation must have *some* effect on the profits of regulated firms. Regulated firms *do* file rate increases that are disallowed, and commissions *do* on occasion order regulated firms to reduce their rates." These are not, however, convincing points. That regulated firms are from time to time forbidden to raise their rates may in some instances signify regulatory error—the agency refusing to allow the firm to cover unavoidably higher costs. In other instances it may simply be the prologue to a deterioration of service. Or it may mean that the firm habitually presents exaggerated requests, knowing the agency will not grant them

[92]This is the conclusion of an empirical study by Stigler & Friedland, *What Can Regulators Regulate? The Case of Electricity*, 5 J. LAW & ECON. 1 (1962), *reprinted in* UTILITY REGULATION: NEW DIRECTIONS IN THEORY AND POLICY 187 (W. Shepherd & T. Gies eds. 1966); *cf.* Pike, *Residential Electric Rates and Regulation*, 7 Q.J. REV. ECON. Bus., Summer 1967, at 45. Curiously, Stigler and Friedland do not discuss the contrary findings of an earlier empirical study that covered much the same ground as they did. *See* TWENTI-ETH CENTURY FUND, ELECTRIC POWER AND GOVERNMENT POLICY: A SURVEY OF THE RELATIONS BETWEEN GOVERNMENT AND THE ELECTRIC POWER INDUSTRY 234–36 (1948). Perhaps that is because the earlier study employs rather primitive empirical techniques and contains a number of obvious deficiencies.

in full. Regulation may be a ritual in which the participants make a noisy but empty show of adversity in order to reassure their respective constituencies of their zeal, and then compromise at a level not far different from what the free market would have dictated.[93]

Orders to reduce rates present the same equivocal aspect. Even without regulatory prodding, a profit-maximizing monopolist would normally reduce rates whenever his costs were reduced (although not by the full amount of the cost reduction), in order to maximize profit under the new cost conditions.[94] But will not shrewd management of a regulated company put up a show of resistance so that the regulatory agency can take credit for having ordered the rate reduction?[95] That will enable the agency to flaunt its effectiveness without impairment of the firm's profits.

[93]I am thus not persuaded by statements like the following: "Many persons—students, scholars, even commissioners—may think that the Bell Company writes up its requests in order to allow for expected Commission reductions in allowable revenue. It makes big claims, in this view, because it expects to settle for much less. In such an opportunistic view of regulatory processes, the company eventually obtains what it really wants and, on the other side, the Commission can show some large paper gains in the interest of telephone buyers. . . . I do not believe that the company men are so deceptive, or the commissioners so naive. Certainly the company may seem to puff up their revenue claims; this is primarily, I think, because they do not make the minimum necessary measures of costs and capital returns. At the same time, the commissioners want to make good regulatory showings in behalf of consumers—and why not?—by using minimal measures of the same costs and the necessary investor returns. But such conflicts in goals do not mean that the regulatory restraints on telephone revenues and prices are not real. The low ratio of Commission approvals of telephone-revenue requests is a meaningful measure of regulatory constraints, and stands as evidence of some regulatory gains for telephone buyers." Troxel, *Telephone Regulation in Michigan*, in UTILITY REGULATION: NEW DIRECTIONS IN THEORY AND POLICY 141, 156–57 (W. Shepherd & T. Gies eds. 1966). The proportion of assertion to reason or evidence in this statement is rather high. It is not that the regulated firm is "deceptive" and the commissioners "naive," but that the firm quite naturally exaggerates its needs in order to provide a generous cushion against commission disallowances and that the commissioners are generally willing to settle for the easy "paper gain" rather than engage in protracted litigation with a company that usually has greater resources for litigation, as well as better access to the facts. At least, this seems to me a plausible view of the regulatory process in operation; calling it "opportunistic" does not make it less so.

If regulation is effective, then I own to some wonderment at the *reported* (which may be much less than the actual) profits of regulated monopolists. In 1967, for example, 39 of the nation's 50 largest utilities had net profits on stockholders' equity, after taxes, of more than 10 percent. Commonwealth Edison, for example, enjoyed a 13.2 percent profit; American Electric Power, 14.9; Panhandle Eastern Pipe Line, 19.1. These examples could be multiplied. *See* FORTUNE, June 15, 1968, at 216–17.

[94]*See* note 57 *supra*.

[95]*See also* text between notes 123 and 124 *infra*.

It is possible that regulatory control of profits is not so ineffectual as suggested. In that event, however, one would be concerned about its effects on the monopolist's incentives to operate efficiently. Suppose a case of perfect profit control. All costs are accurately determined, including the cost of equity capital; the rate base is accurately valued; and costs and valuation are continuously updated. The firm's overall revenue requirements are equated to its cost of service and continuously revised upward or downward with any rise or fall in that cost. There would be no monopoly profits under such a regime, but neither would there be any incentive on the part of the monopolist to improve his efficiency. Lacking either the "stick" of competitive pressure or the "carrot" of supracompetitive profits, the managers of the firm would have no reason to strive for better performance save their own pride or professionalism. While such factors should not be underestimated, so drastic an alteration of the structure of incentives operating on a monopolistic firm would be an exorbitant price to pay for the elimination of monopoly profits.

One can reply that the problem of incentives is solved by the accident of regulatory lag—and solved in a way that preserves a large measure of regulatory effectiveness in limiting the monopolist's profits. Rates are periodically, not continuously, equated with costs, and this procedure limits without absolutely foreclosing the monopolist's opportunity to extract supracompetitive profits; for in the periods between regulatory determinations the regulated firm has a profit incentive to become more efficient. Regulatory lag may not, however, be a complete answer to the incentive problem. In the first place, it is an inadvertent method of injecting a profit incentive. While it permits supranormal profits to be obtained, there is no express recognition that they are legitimate and acceptable as a method of encouraging a monopolist to better his performance. I have considerable doubt, however, whether this inexplicitness makes any practical difference. More important, one cannot be sure that the opportunity provided by regulatory lag to obtain monopoly profits is sufficient to avoid serious disincentive effects, albeit those effects might be even greater were there no lag. If the regulated firm achieves a technical breakthrough that enables it to reduce its costs and increase its profits substantially, the regulatory agency, if reasonably alert, will move with dispatch as the firm's rate of return begins to climb. The regulated firm will enjoy some profits in the interim, but they may be less than without regulation—conceivably so much less as to diminish the firm's interest in pursuing future break-throughs. It is striking to observe that regulatory agencies appear not even to make a distinction between profits derived from the exploitation of a patented device or process and other monopoly profits.[96] An effectively regulated firm, then, may be denied the minimum reward for inventive activity that a competitive firm would obtain and that society deems essential to elicit adequate innovation.

I do not argue that a monopolist's incentive to efficient and progressive operation is necessarily diminished by *any* curtailment of the amount of profits it can obtain from improved performance. But it would not follow that one could practicably limit the profits of a monopolist without impairing his incentives. There are two difficulties. First, it is no easy trick to determine the level at which one can be confident that there will be no significant disincentive effects. The difficulty is sufficiently indicated by asking, by way of analogy, whether a ceiling of $50,000 on individual incomes would have such effects. The second and, I think, critical point is that even a rather high ceiling on profits might well reduce a monopolist's *inventive* activity. Those who argue that competitive firms are likely to innovate more rapidly than monopolists point out that the competitive firm is motivated by a desire to obtain and exploit a monopoly, which the monopolist already has. I indicated earlier my view that this difference is probably unimportant, in part because the monopolist can obtain very large profits from a successful innovation, especially one that creates an improved or different product. If, however, regulation curtails the monopolist's ability to profit from innovation, it may impair his incentive to innovate. Given the cardinal importance of technological advance to economic welfare, and the fact that regulation includes no techniques for inducing a regulated firm to innovate at an optimal rate, this point argues strongly against profit controls.

One could argue that any disincentive effects of profit regulation are likely to be offset by the pressure that it may be thought to place on the regulated firm to keep its costs down in a period, such as the present, when costs generally are rising due to inflation. The regulatory agency may be reluctant to allow rate increases; or regulatory lag may operate to prevent the firm from placing new rates in effect

[96] I do not include cases in which the regulated firm obtains royalties from licensing its patent to companies in other lines of business; such royalties are presumably excluded from the computation of revenues derived from the regulated service and hence subject to limitation by the regulatory agency.

promptly. It behooves the firm, therefore, to economize wherever possible. I am inclined to doubt the importance of this effect. First, I sense no general tendency of regulatory agencies to refuse justified rate increases. Moreover, commonly the firm is entitled to place a rate increase in effect after a brief suspension period, subject only to a duty to refund should the increase eventually be found to have been unwarranted. Second, a firm denied a justified rate increase usually has a simple remedy that does not require any economizing: to reduce the quality of its output. Third, the incentive effect that we are discussing is operative only when the cost trend in the regulated industry is upward. Even in highly inflationary periods, this condition will not always hold. Not all industries are equally affected by inflation, and in some technological progress or other factors may completely offset any inflationary pressures. Despite the general upward cost trend in the economy, costs have been falling throughout much of the regulated sector for many years.

Finally, even if it is true that regulation often prevents a regulated firm from automatically covering any cost increase by raising its rates, an unregulated monopolist is in a quite comparable position. A monopolist whose costs increase will raise his price, but not by the full amount of the increase; and at the new price his profits will be less than before the cost increase.[97] Recall, too, our point that the current owners of a monopoly firm receive only normal profits, the monopoly profits being discounted in the current price of the firm's stock. If we join these two observations, we see that a cost increase will reduce an unregulated monopolist's profits and that the profit reduction will hurt. In sum, profit regulation reduces the reward to the monopolist of superior performance without, it would seem, materially increasing the penalty for failing to minimize costs.

Another way in which profit regulation could have pernicious side effects, besides generally deadening incentive, is by encouraging excessive expansion of plant.[98] If the profits of a regulated firm

[97]This can be seen from the diagram in note 57 *supra*. Suppose the firm's costs are MC' and they increase to MC. It is readily apparent that at the new profit-maximizing price (p) the firm's profits are less than they were at p', the profit-maximizing price under cost conditions MC.

[98]*See* Averch & Johnson, *Behavior of the Firm Under Regulatory Constraint*, 52 AM. ECON. REV. 1052 (1962); Wellisz, *Regulation of Natural Gas Pipeline Companies: An Economic Analysis*, 71 J. POL. ECON, 30 (1963). For an early intuition of this effect see Cabot, *Public Utility Rate Regulation* 1, 7 HARV. BUS. REV. 257, 259 (1929).

are effectively constrained but at a level exceeding the true cost of capital, the firm cannot obtain additional profits by reducing its costs but it can by expanding its rate base. Let the true cost of capital to regulated firm X be 7 percent and the allowed rate of return 8 percent. X will make no additional profit by reducing its cost of operation for we have assumed that its profits are effectively constrained at the allowed rate, and that implies that any cost reduction will be promptly reflected in a corresponding rate reduction. On the other hand, by building a new plant for $1 million X will earn a monopoly profit of $10,000 per year (1(8-7) percent of $1 million) whether or not it can sell the plant's output at a price that covers cost. The plant may be grossly inefficient, producing widgets at a cost of 5 cents apiece when the highest price that can be obtained for a widget is 3 cents; it doesn't matter. The annual cost of the plant is added to X's overall cost of service and its overall revenue requirements are increased by that amount. X will have to increase price in some other market in order to cover its revenue requirements at the new level, because the revenue from the new plant is insufficient to cover the plant's costs; but that should be no problem. If, as assumed, X's profits are effectively constrained, albeit at a higher level than the true cost of capital, X must have unexploited monopoly power that it can use to raise prices to cover a higher level of revenue requirements.

The theory is logical but requires qualification to be realistic. First, we should not assume that excess profits can be obtained *only* by capital expansion. If through operation of regulatory lag, or because monopoly profits can be disguised as items of cost, the monopolist has opportunities for increasing profits by minimizing cost, inefficient capital expansion becomes of questionable advantage. The monopolist may find it more advantageous to economize on all costs, including capital costs, and to take advantage of regulatory lag or accounting loopholes to realize the cost savings as profit. How these considerations trade off will vary from case to case.

Second, the conscious pursuit of inefficient capital policies by a monopolist could engender crises of managerial psychology and company esprit de corps. It would require managers to admit, at least to themselves, that the allowed rate of return exceeded the firm's true cost of capital—contrary to the position that management invariably takes in regulatory proceedings. More important, one may doubt whether a firm could hope to attract and hold competent and responsible project managers, comptrollers, engineers, and

63

other essential personnel if it told them to throw out notions of efficiency and design systems that inefficiently consumed large amounts of capital. Any firm that succeeded in indoctrinating its personnel with precepts of inefficiency, moreover, would gravely undermine its ability to respond to potential competition, a threat that can never be ruled out entirely. In sum, here is an area where an assumption of blind short-run profit maximization would be unrealistic. To make some additional profits, management would be discarding efficiency as a guiding principle for its employees, would be acting unprofessionally, would be undermining its position in regulatory proceedings, and would be impairing its capacity to anticipate and repel new entrants.

On the other hand, it is entirely possible that a capital-expansive bias might operate on an unconscious level. Sensing that capital costs did not have the same impact on profitability as operating expenses, management in a close case might choose an owned over a leased facility, a flat rate that encouraged use of its facilities and hence required their expansion over a capital-conserving peak surcharge, a plant with heavy initial cost but light maintenance over a less expensive plant that would require greater outlays for maintenance over its lifetime, excessive backup or "fail safe" devices, zero queuing, and so on—many of these being practices dear to the engineer's heart anyway. Even assuming that the bias operates only in the close case, the cumulative inefficiencies traceable to it could be quite substantial.

Persuasive evidence of capital-expansive bias has not turned up.[99] But then no systematic empirical study has yet been attempted. And we have just seen that the bias is likely to operate, if at all, in close cases where it will be difficult or impossible to detect.

Regulation may encourage other wasteful expenditures. Management can react in two ways to a ceiling on profits. It can charge the price that will return the allowed profit and no more. Or it can charge the monopoly price but convert the forbidden profit into increased cost. The latter is the course that managerial self-interest could be expected to dictate. In its crudest but from the standpoint of efficiency

---

[99]*See* Shepherd, *Regulatory Constraints and Public Utility Investment,* 42 LAND ECON. 348 (1966). There is some suggestive (but no more than that) evidence in Wein, *Fair Rate of Return and Incentives—Some General Considerations,* in PERFORMANCE UNDER REGULATION 39, 48–53 (H. Trebing ed. 1968), and Westfield, *Regulation and Conspiracy,* 55 AM. ECON. REV. 424 (1965).

least injurious form managerial self-interest would manifest itself in the payment of excessive salaries to managers. Since executive salary is formally a cost, the firm would not appear to exceed its profit constraint. However, the transfer of profits to management in the form of exorbitant salaries is one kind of evasive maneuver that a regulatory agency is likely to be able to detect. Consequently, conversion of monopoly profits into management perquisites would be likely to assume less transparent forms. In addition to the important category of expenditures discussed next—those designed to generate political favor for the firm—such transmuted profits could show up as superfluous staff (increasing managerial self-importance), luxurious quarters, the avoidance of uncongenial (but efficient) personnel, and in many other forms. One cannot dismiss such costs as mere rents equivalent to the monopoly profits that the managers might prefer to capture directly. The perquisites obtained by such expenditures may represent distinctly second-best choices, resulting in a less efficient use of resources than if the managers (or the stockholders or consumers) had received an equivalent amount of money directly. And I would emphasize that this point does not depend on any assumption that corporate managers do not wish to maximize profit. The managers of an effectively regulated firm cannot maximize profit. They must choose between maximizing consumers' welfare and their own. Assuming that individuals are principally motivated by self-interest, the latter option is the likelier to be exercised.[100]

A further troublesome aspect of profit regulation is that it may encourage management in some instances to subordinate efficiency to winning political support and public goodwill for the firm's objectives. Regulation places a firm in continuous, rather than merely intermittent or extraordinary, confrontation with a government agency that has potentially far-reaching power over the firm's welfare. A corporate leader blessed with "statesmanlike" vision—or, if you prefer, a maximizer of profit in the long rather than merely the short run—will be tempted to seize opportunities to enhance the firm's security by measures whether or not economically justified that are designed to placate the agency or the political forces to which the agency is sensitive. The greater the government's involvement in the firm's activities and fortunes, the greater will be the

[100]For some suggestive, although again far from conclusive, empirical support see Alchian & Kessel, *Competition, Monopoly, and the Pursuit of Money*, in ASPECTS OF LABOR ECONOMICS 157 (Nat'l Bureau Econ. Research 1962).

firm's incentive to pursue policies designed to create a favorable climate of political opinion toward the firm even at some sacrifice in immediate profit maximization through cost minimization. The firm will have an incentive, for example, to make generous settlements with its employees, who are probably represented by a politically influential union;[101] to protect inefficient competitors—who may have substantial political influence—by umbrella pricing; and to give favorable treatment, in respects such as price and plant location, to communities or regions where important political support is at stake.

To some extent, tendencies of this sort may be held in check by the same considerations that should temper conscious indulgence of capital-expansive tendencies—the professional self-respect that provides essential cement in any large and bureaucratic organization. However, managers may understand and accept the necessity to temper strict profit considerations with political reality—with "statesmanship"—more readily than they could accept the necessity or propriety of deliberately squandering capital in recognition that the regulatory agency might be allowing the firm more than a fair return on capital.[102]

These reflections undermine the common notion that, however ineffectual in practice, regulation is a wholesome influence on the behavior of the regulated firm because the firm knows that if it performs poorly the regulatory screws may be tightened. I grant—in fact claim—that a rational management will follow a behavior pattern designed to dominate or appease the regulatory agency. What is not clear is whether such a pattern will usually promote the welfare of society as a whole. As the political scientists have reminded us, the regulatory agencies are a part of the political process;[103] and while it

[101]But recall our qualification concerning the effect on efficiency. *See* text accompanying note 52 *supra*.

[102]There is some interesting, although unfortunately rather dated, evidence that the telephone and electric utilities engage in a number of the activities discussed in text. *See* INVESTIGATION OF THE TELEPHONE INDUSTRY IN THE UNITED STATES, H.R. Doc. No. 340, 76th Cong., 1st Sess. 118, 475–89 (1939); I. BARNES, THE ECONOMICS OF PUBLIC UTILITY REGULATION 782–815 (1942), and sources cited therein. On the other hand, the Twentieth Century Fund's study of the electric power industry found that the costs of regulated utilities were lower than those of unregulated utilities during the period studied. TWENTIETH CENTURY FUND, *supra* note 92, at 241.

[103]*See, e.g.*, M. BERNSTEIN, REGULATING BUSINESS BY INDEPENDENT COMMISSION (1955); E. REDFORD, ADMINISTRATION OF NATIONAL ECONOMIC CONTROL (1952); Fainsod, *Some*

would be pleasant to suppose that regulated firms considered cost minimization and avoidance of monopoly profits to be the surest paths to accommodation with regulators, any such supposition would impute to them an improbable political innocence. Cost minimization and profit avoidance require hard bargaining with employees' representatives, refusal to serve customers unable to pay the cost of serving them, refusal to give preferential treatment to politically influential firms or localities, and other policies likely to be highly unpopular with precisely those groups that can bring the strongest pressure to bear on the legislature and, either through it or directly, on the regulators. Consumers are the least organized and therefore typically the least effective interest group. The long-run consumer interest in particular has no lobby.[104]

It is, to be sure, a fair question whether eliminating regulation would cure these tendencies. Monopolists would still not want to give offense to politically powerful groups, lest regulation be reimposed or other measures taken against them. However, restrictive legislation is rarely imposed on an industry (without its connivance) unless dramatic abuses of one sort or another can be demonstrated. A competently managed monopolist would probably not generate that kind of evidence.

Let us turn to another area in which profit regulation may have harmful side effects. It was noted earlier that the determination of cost of service is fraught with uncertainty. That will not always result in the agency's overestimating the regulated firm's revenue requirements. Occasionally the agency may prevent the regulated firm from fixing a level of prices that covers its costs. The agency may underestimate the cost of capital and thereby impair the firm's ability to finance needed plant expansions[105] unless by some evasive maneuver (for example, degrading service) the firm is able to avoid the impact of the agency's ruling. The same result will follow if the agency improperly disallows a claimed item of expense (again assuming no

---

Reflections on the Nature of the Regulatory Process, in 1 PUBLIC POLICY 297 (C. Friedrich & E. Mason eds. 1940).

[104]For a persuasive explanation of why relatively small groups do well at the expense of large when resources are allocated through the political process see M. OLSON, THE LOGIC OF COLLECTIVE ACTION: PUBLIC GOODS AND THE THEORY OF GROUPS (1965).

[105]*See, e.g.,* J. HIRSHLEIFER, J. DE HAVEN & J. MILLIMAN, WATER SUPPLY: ECONOMICS, TECHNOLOGY, AND POLICY 109–11 (1960).

evasion by the regulated firm). Such errors can distort the allocation of resources as badly as excessive prices.

An interesting variant of this problem has occurred in industries involved in the extraction of depletable resources, such as natural gas. The price of such a resource should include a noncost component—economic rent—designed to ration the use of the resource and prevent its depletion before adequate substitute resources are available.[106] But the inclusion of economic rent, which is not a cost in any obvious or conventional sense and which swells the profits of the regulated firm, is superficially difficult to reconcile with the notion that profits must be limited to cost of service. The Federal Power Commission, in its regulation of the interstate rates of natural gas producers, has refused to allow the inclusion of a rent factor in producers' rates.[107] This decision could produce a highly inefficient pattern of exploitation of the resource, although severance taxes, allowed as costs, may perform the rationing function to some extent.

Even if all costs and scarcity rents are properly determined, a rate based thereon may be too low and cause inefficient allocation of resources. Suppose, by way of an admittedly crude example, that widgets cost 8 cents to produce and are sold by a monopolist at 11 cents and that zidgets cost 7 cents to produce and are sold by their producers, who for one reason or another enjoy substantial market power, for 9 cents. For some potential widget customers, widgets have no adequate substitutes, so they are not tempted by the lower-priced zidget; but for others the zidget is a perfectly adequate substitute, and since zidgets are lower-priced than widgets this class of customers buys zidgets. Now suppose that the widget industry is brought under regulation and the regulatory agency compels the monopolist to reduce his price to his cost. Those for whom zidgets are interchangeable with widgets will switch to widgets, since the price of a zidget, 9 cents, is higher than the new widget price, 8 cents (equal to its cost). But the switch is to a more costly substitute (zidgets cost only 7 cents to produce). Expanding the widget output at

---

[106]*See* Note, *Regulation of Depletable Resource Industries,* 19 STAN. L. REV. 1036 (1967); *cf.* Hotelling, *The Economics of Exhaustible Resources,* 39 J. POL. ECON. 137 (1931); Pabst, *Unstable Conditions of Competition and Monopoly in Exhaustible Resource Industries,* 50 J. POL. ECON. 739 (1942).

[107]*See* Area Rate Proceeding No. AR61-1, 34 F.P.C. 159 (1965), *upheld in* Permian Basin Area Rate Cases, 390 U.S. 747 (1968). For a glimmering of awareness that price might have an important rationing function in this industry see FPC v. Hope Natural Gas Co., 320 U.S. 591, 657–59 (1944) (separate opinion of Jackson, J.).

the expense of the zidget output wastes resources; the agency should not have reduced the widget price below 9 cents, even though at that price the seller would still be obtaining monopoly profits. In very few cases, however, will the correct "second best" solution, that is, a solution that takes proper account of the existence of cost-price disparities in other sectors of the economy, be determinable. Regulatory efforts to eliminate monopoly profits may, therefore, if effective, often create fresh distortions in resource allocation.

Finally, regulation of profits creates an incentive for the regulated firm to diversify, regardless of efficiency considerations, into markets that are unregulated or laxly regulated; for diversification may enable it to evade the constraint of regulation. If a regulated company owns an equipment manufacturer (the usual pattern in the telephone industry) it can transfer monopoly profits from the regulated to the nonregulated market simply by raising equipment prices to itself.[108] Similar opportunities are presented if, as is common in the gas, electrical, and telephone industries, the regulated firm incurs joint or common costs in the provision of various services that are not all regulated or are regulated by separate agencies that differ in regulatory capability or strictness.[109] Allocation of joint or common costs among services is not merely difficult; it is inherently arbitrary.[110] Short of radically curtailing the scope of regulated firms' operations, possibly at great sacrifice in efficiency, or completely revamping the existing division of regulatory responsibilities between the federal government and the states, there is no way to eliminate the tactical advantage that a diversified or integrated firm enjoys in sparring with the regulators. This observation has disquieting implications. In the absence of regulation one could assume that monopolists generally would not enter other markets unless they could operate efficiently there. Such an assumption cannot be indulged, however, if by expanding the scope of its operations the monopolist can complicate and perhaps defeat the regulators' attempts to limit his profits.

[108]For efforts by regulatory agencies to prevent any such transfer see, *e.g.,* Pacific Tel. & Tel. Co., 23 P.U.R.3d 209 (Cal. Pub. Util. Comm. 1958); Southwestern Bell Tel. Co., 92 P.U.R. (N.S.) 481 (Mo. Pub. Serv. Comm. 1952).

[109]*See, e.g.,* FPC v. United Gas Pipe Line Co., 386 U.S. 237 (1967); R. GABEL, *supra* note 91.

[110]*See* Johnson, *Joint Cost and Price Discrimination: The Case of Communications Satellites,* 37 J. BUS. U. CHI. 32 (1964), *reprinted in* UTILITY REGULATION: NEW DIRECTIONS IN THEORY AND POLICY 117, 133–34 (W. Shepherd & T. Gies eds. 1966).

What our discussion of the pernicious side effects of profit regulation crucially implies is that if an attempt is made to limit a company's profits the government must also concern itself with dimensions of firm behavior that could otherwise be left to the free market, such as the efficiency with which the firm employs capital and other resources, the rate and direction of its inventive activity, its expansion into other markets, and (a point to be discussed next) the structure of its prices. These are areas in which a natural monopolist, left to itself, might be expected at least to approximate satisfactory performance. Once its profits are constrained—even partially—the monopolist's incentives to economically efficient and progressive performance are distorted, and much broader regulatory controls of company activity become necessary. Regulatory agencies theoretically impose such controls, but, as will appear, the practice is rather different. In an effort, very possibly doomed to essential futility, to control monopoly profits, regulation fosters other and potentially more serious harms that it is largely incapable of controlling.

2. *Regulation of rate structure and entry.*

Regulatory commissions control the level and relationship of specific rates by virtue of their authority to forbid unjust, unreasonable, or unjustly discriminatory rates. They also control entry into regulated markets, since to provide regulated services a firm must obtain a certificate of public convenience and necessity. These powers— over specific rates and over entry—are best discussed together, since they are highly interdependent.

It was implicit in an earlier discussion that an inefficient pricing structure is not a certain or even likely result of natural monopoly, except that the natural monopolist, even if he discriminates, may restrict output somewhat.[111] The unregulated monopolist who desires to maximize profit will have an incentive to sell to any customer prepared to pay the minimum cost of serving that customer but he will not sell below that cost, for that would be a losing proposition. And yet there is a good deal of evidence that grossly inefficient pricing is widespread in the regulated industries. For example, a striking characteristic of the rate structures of regulated companies is the frequency with which the costs of providing different services or of providing the same service in different areas are averaged together and

[111]*See* text accompanying notes 45–49 *supra.*

a single rate charged that appreciably exceeds the cost of serving some customers and is far below that of serving others. The charge for a long-distance telephone call of a given distance and duration is the same everywhere in the continental United States even though it is plain that differences of terrain and density make costs on different routes vary widely (often, I am informed by industry sources, by as much as 10 to 1).[112] Similarly, urban telephone rates are widely believed not to reflect the lower costs due to greater population density of serving urban as compared to rural residents. Passenger service is commonly provided by railroads at rates far below the cost of the service.[113] These examples could be multiplied.[114]

The establishment of broad rate categories that inevitably give some consumers a windfall and overcharge others to the point of deterring them from taking service may be partly justified by the added accounting and metering expenses that a more discriminating structure would require. Tariff schedules are typically quite complex anyway and it may be costly to make them more so. But that is not a complete explanation. It does not explain why railroads provide passenger service on a subsidized basis or why the Bell System charges rural customers less than urban even though this apparently involves a subsidy of the former by the latter. Nor can the entire explanation be managerial ignorance of price theory. And as already noted it is not commercial self-interest in any obvious sense that leads regulated firms to provide service at a loss—witness the number of abandonment proceedings in the passenger-train business.[115] I suspect that the heart of the problem may be regulation itself.

The essence of a public utility's or common carrier's duty, as traditionally conceived, is to serve all comers at fair rates.[116] While a harmless enough concept, which does not necessarily imply a duty to provide service at rates below cost, it has seemed to many to support the proposition that regulated service should be provided on a universal basis at uniform rates. That proposition has never carried

---

[112]For an excellent discussion of telephone ratemaking see L. JOHNSON, COMMUNICATIONS SATELLITES AND TELEPHONE RATES: PROBLEMS OF GOVERNMENT REGULATION (RAND Corp. RM-2845-NASA Oct. 1961).

[113]See, e.g., M. CONANT, RAILROAD MERGERS AND ABANDONMENTS 132 (1964).

[114]See, e.g., J. MEYER, J. KAIN & M. WOHL, THE URBAN TRANSPORTATION PROBLEM 357 (1965).

[115]See M. CONANT, supra note 113, at 113–65.

[116]For a recent affirmation of this principle see American Trucking Ass'ns v. Atchison, T. & S.F. Ry., 387 U.S. 397, 406–07 (1967).

the day completely. Refusals to serve are not uncommon. The existence of the Rural Electrification Administration, with its continuing programs of assistance to rural telephone as well as rural electrical cooperatives, sufficiently attests to that. But it has been influential, to say the least.[117] The public has been led to expect that, except in really outlandish locations, utility services will be available to all at close to a standard level. In the language of one commentator, "a utility must take the 'lean with the fat.' While it provides some unprofitable but necessary service to the public, it recoups the loss from the profits of other operations."[118]

Thus, while the regulatory agencies may not be very effective in eliminating monopoly pricing by regulated firms, they have succeeded in compelling the firms to use a portion of their profits to subsidize the extension of regulated service to those who would not pay a remunerative rate. Superficially an attractive idea, on reflection internal subsidization is seen to have a number of questionable features. In the first place, a subsidy of a service rather than of money—a subsidy in kind, as it were—limits consumer choice. We may find it difficult to conceive of doing without telephone or air-transport service, but the residents of northern Maine or rural Alabama may have different priorities. It might be more sensible to give these people some of the added tax revenues that would be obtained from the utilities and carriers were they not required to conduct losing operations and to let each individual decide whether he needed better communications, better transportation—or better housing or better food.

In the second place, internal subsidization is an incredibly crude instrument for assisting needy or deserving elements of society. All too often, the principal beneficiaries turn out to be members of the affluent middle class. Urban telephone revenues apparently subsidize suburban service, although it is generally the poor who live in the city and the well-to-do who live in the suburbs. Suburban commuters are among those who chiefly benefit from below-cost passenger-train rates. A consistent social goal is difficult to discern beneath the complicated and shifting pattern of internal subsidies in the regulated industries. It seems doubtful that direct subsidies would miss the mark so often by so much.

[117]Some of its effects in the railroad industry are discussed in J. HILLMAN, COMPETITION AND RAILROAD PRICE DISCRIMINATION (1968).

[118]J. BAUER, EFFECTIVE REGULATION OF PUBLIC UTILITIES 17–18 (1925).

Worse, internal subsidies give a stamp of legitimacy and propriety to monopoly profits independent of natural monopoly, and thereby help to entrench the regulated monopolist. (That may be why the Bell System, the most astute of regulated enterprises in dealing with government, is an ardent proponent of the principle of taking the lean with the fat.) When used to subsidize a worthy cause, monopoly profits become quite respectable, and remain so even after the markets in which they are obtained have ceased to be natural monopolies. What is more, if the regulated firm's monopoly position is eroded by competitors, the subsidy program will have to look elsewhere for support. Internal subsidization thus enables a regulated firm, seconded by the beneficiaries of its internal subsidies, to argue to the regulators that they should use their control over new entry to preserve its monopoly despite changed conditions of cost and demand, and to denounce prospective entrants into its monopoly markets as "cream skimmers" who by competing away the firm's monopoly profits would cut the ground out from under its subsidized customers in other markets. Entry is frequently denied on this ground.[119] Nor is the ground a frivolous one—if, that is, internal subsidization is embraced as desirable social policy. Entry into the regulated firm's monopoly markets by other firms *will* undermine the subsidy program. It is *not* altogether fair to make it compete against a "cream skimmer" when it must support losing operations in other markets while the cream skimmer bears no such burden.

Finally, internal subsidies promote misallocation of resources. An inefficient competitor may be attracted to a regulated market by the fact that the monopolist is maintaining so large a spread between his costs and his rates in that market (in order to subsidize below-cost service elsewhere) that the entrant can make a profit even though his cost of service is higher than the incumbent's. That is, the monopolist's responsibilities in other markets may prevent it from reducing its price to forestall threatened entry. In these circumstances, price

[119]*See* J. MEYER, M. PECK, J. STENASON & C. ZWICK, THE ECONOMICS OF COMPETITION IN THE TRANSPORTATION INDUSTRIES 249 (1959). For a recent case where entry was denied on "cream skimming" grounds see Authorized Entities and Authorized Users Under the Communications Satellite Act of 1962, 4 F.C.C.2d 421, 431–33 (1966). For a dramatic example of the effect on rates of new entry into a "lush" market see Comment, *Is Regulation Necessary? California Air Transportation and National Regulatory Policy,* 74 YALE L.J. 1416, 1432–39 (1965), describing how entry of a "cream skimmer" on the Los Angeles-San Francisco route caused rates in the market to fall to less than one-half the rate from Boston to Washington, a comparable distance.

cannot fulfill its function of directing resources to the areas where they can be employed most efficiently; rather, it invites wasteful duplication. Internal subsidies, then, create a danger of misallocation of resources, and that danger, in turn, provides additional justification for regulatory control over entry.

The strongest argument *for* internal subsidization is that the regulated services are so fundamental that if the companies had not subsidized their extension throughout the land government would probably have done so and—the political process being what it is—at even higher levels.[120] Yet, when one considers how many genuine essentials are not subsidized, it is far from clear that the "lean with the fat" principle of regulation actually headed off an extravagant program of government subsidies. And at all events, it is pure conjecture that the added cost (if any) of direct subsidy (if any) would have exceeded the considerable social costs that have in fact resulted from endeavors to prevent cream skimming. To illustrate, in the 19th century the railroad industry extended service at very low rates to many areas in the Western United States. The growth of competing modes of transportation in subsequent years, especially trucking, eroded the monopoly profits out of which the low Western rates had been subsidized. The efficient response of the railroads would have been to raise those rates (as demand conditions evidently warranted). But a great many business enterprises had been attracted to the West in reliance on the low rates, and they had sufficient influence with Congress and the Interstate Commerce Commission not only to prevent the needed revision in rail rates but also to bring trucking under regulation, lest truck competition completely erode the railroads' pattern of preferential rates.[121] We should be reminded by this example that internal subsidization through regulation is not a complete escape from politics. On the contrary, regulation, to repeat an earlier point, is inescapably a part of the political

[120]For a recent empirical study of the tendency toward overinvestment in public projects see J. BAIN, R. CAVES & J. MARGOLIS, NORTHERN CALIFORNIA'S WATER INDUSTRY: THE COMPARATIVE EFFICIENCY OF PUBLIC ENTERPRISE IN DEVELOPING A SCARCE NATURAL RESOURCE (1966). For a theoretical explanation of why this should be so see J. BUCHANAN & G. TULLOCK, THE CALCULUS OF CONSENT: LOGICAL FOUNDATIONS OF CONSTITUTIONAL DEMOCRACY 131–45, 164, 289–91 (1962).

[121]*See* Nelson & Greiner, *The Relevance of the Common Carrier Under Modern Economic Conditions,* in TRANSPORTATION ECONOMICS 352, 356–64 (Nat'l Bureau Econ. Research 1965).

process. It is not surprising, therefore, that a regulated rate structure should bear the imprint of political pressures at some cost in efficiency.

Internal subsidization is one seeming example of the perverse effect of regulation on pricing efficiency; another is tardiness in offering promotional rates. While the demand for a monopolist's product or service will be less responsive to price changes than the demand facing each firm in a competitive market, it will not be completely unresponsive, and large profits may reward a search for areas in which lower rates will evoke substantial additional revenues at little additional cost. Assume that an electric utility must build a very large plant in order to meet peak-hour demands for electricity but in off-peak hours much of the plant stands idle. Since fixed costs (costs that are independent of whether the plant is generating or not) bulk large in a utility's total costs, the utility can afford to provide off-peak service at much lower rates than peak service. The peak customers will defray the company's entire fixed costs, and if it can attract off-peak customers at rates that at least cover its variable costs of production it will make additional profits.[122] One would expect, therefore, that natural monopolists would be keen to explore areas where additional customers could be attracted by reduced rates. Although promotional rates are a common feature of the rate structures of regulated companies, observers find that regulated firms have not really exploited the opportunities for tailoring their rates to varying demands.[123] Part of the reason may be ignorance of price theory by managers and part may be the accounting and metering costs associated with complex rate structures; but part I suspect again is regulation.

[122] A low off-peak rate should be distinguished from a discriminatory rate. One can argue that since the size of plant is determined by peak use it is not discriminatory to make the peak users bear the entire overhead; those are all costs of serving *them*. *See* Hirshleifer, *Peak Loads and Efficient Pricing: Comment*, 72 Q.J. ECON. 451 (1958). Promotional rates may also be discriminatory, in the sense of being based on an allocation of overhead expenses that has nothing to do with relative costs but only with relative elasticities of demand. But we saw earlier that price discrimination may permit more efficient utilization of capacity. *See* text accompanying notes 45–49 *supra*.

[123] *See, e.g.*, R. DAVIDSON, PRICE DISCRIMINATION IN SELLING GAS AND ELECTRICITY 217–18 (1955); Rosenberg, *Natural-Gas–Pipeline Rate Regulation: Marginal-Cost Pricing and the Zone-Allocation Problem*, 75 J. POL. ECON. 159 (1967); Shepherd, *Marginal-Cost Pricing in American Industries*, 23 S. ECON. J. 58 (1966); Vickrey, *Pricing in Urban and Suburban Transport*, in READINGS IN URBAN TRANSPORTATION 120 (G. Smerk ed. 1968).

Promotional price reductions and other marketing innovations are, in their initial stages, experiments, for consumer response cannot be gauged accurately by prior analysis. A firm may be reluctant to undertake such an experiment if it has reason to believe that the commission may be sticky about permitting a rate increase should the company judge the experiment a failure. Moreover, a firm may prefer to be prodded by the agency to reduce rates in price-elastic areas in the hope that, if the reduction results in an overall increase in revenues and profits, it will stand a better chance of being permitted to keep them.

What is involved in this last example is a subtle method of avoiding the impact of a commission order that the firm revise its rate schedule to reduce overall profits. If the firm responds by reducing rates to a level at which, applied to current output, they would yield no more than the total revenue requirements allowed by the commission, but in fact the reduced rates stimulate demand and produce a higher level of revenue, the firm, as a result of regulatory lag, may avoid the impact of the commission's order. It will also have an effective argument against the prompt initiation of a new proceeding. It was ordered to reduce rates and did so. If through its ingenuity the rate reduction actually enhanced its profits, everyone is better off. Why should it be penalized by a new proceeding? The added profit and the argument would be foreclosed to the firm if it explored all possible areas of elastic demand before the rate proceeding was held.

There is an additional reason why regulated companies may be sluggish about experimenting with promotional rates. Insofar as the regulatory process limits the overall profits of the firm, it reduces the rewards of efficient pricing. The unregulated monopolist who avoids promotional ratemaking in any market is throwing money away. He cannot make up the lost profits by raising prices in another market, for he will already be charging all the traffic will bear in every one of his markets. But if profit regulation is at all effective there will be unexploited monopoly profits available to cover any missed profit opportunities caused by failure to tailor particular rates to particular cost and demand conditions.

Many pricing inefficiencies under regulation arise, finally, from regulatory efforts to control competition. The tools of control are two: the certificating power, which enables the regulatory agency to prevent entry of competitors into a regulated market; and the power to fix minimum rates, which enables the regulatory agency to limit price competition among the firms permitted in the market. As previously noted, both powers derive a part of their justification from a desire to maintain patterns of internal subsidization that competition could destroy. Primarily, however, the rationale of regulating entry is that unlimited entry under conditions of natural monopoly leads to ruinous competition, and of minimum rate regulation that a monopolistic firm is likely to employ predatory price discrimination against other sellers.

As explained earlier, the fear of ruinous competition seems largely groundless.[124] If a prospective entrant realizes there is room for only one firm in the market, it will not enter unless confident of being able to supplant the existing monopolist. If it enters in the mistaken belief that the market will support more than one seller or that it is more efficient than the incumbent, it will soon be eliminated either by bankruptcy or by being acquired (presumably at a low price, reflecting its poor prospects) by the incumbent. So long as a single firm can meet the market's entire demand most efficiently, one can be reasonably confident that the market will shake down to a single firm, at least if there are no undue inhibitions on price competition or merger.

But limitations on entry are worse than superfluous; they constitute a barrier to entry that may perpetuate monopoly long after a market has ceased to be naturally monopolistic. A firm that reckons that cost conditions are now favorable to entry must convince a government agency of the fact. That will require a formal submission, substantial legal and related expenses, and a delay often of years— all before the firm may commence operations. The costs and delay are alone enough to discourage many a prospective entrant. Much more is involved than running a procedural gauntlet, however, for ultimate success is by no means certain. The favor with which regulatory agencies look upon entry varies with the agency and the period, but the predominant inclination has been negative; there is now

---

[124]*See* text preceding note 70 *supra*. Perhaps there is some danger that a firm might enter a natural monopoly market for the sole purpose of inducing the incumbent monopolist to buy it out; this might lead to overbuilding. One would judge this a highly risky strategy, however, requiring as it would the sinking of substantial costs in a venture quite likely to end in disaster. Concern with this possibility hardly seems a sufficient basis for the regulation of entry into natural monopoly markets.

a good deal of evidence that the certificating power has been used to limit greatly the growth of competition in the regulated industries.[125]

The only justification for regulating entry that seems at all appealing (putting aside the special case noted earlier of internal subsidies that may create misleading price signals) is that a true market test of a new entrant's efficiency may fail to materialize due to the regulatory agency's power to prescribe minimum rates.[126] Once a prospective entrant has persuaded the agency to allow it to enter a regulated market, regulation ceases to be a barrier to the new firm and becomes a shield. If the incumbent reduces his rates to meet the competition of the newcomer, the latter can challenge the rate reduction before the commission as unfairly low—an abuse of monopoly power. By invoking the minimum-rate power, the entrant stands a fair chance of blocking even legitimate price responses, and hence of surviving despite being inefficient. This is because regulatory agencies traditionally abhor discriminatory pricing, even when wholly appropriate as a competitive response; and because practical administrative guidelines for nonpredatory competitive price responses are elusive, which may lead the agency to limit such responses unduly.

In a previous example we saw that it was efficient for railroad R to lower its coal rates to $12.50 per ton to meet the competition of R', even though the result was that R was charging $17.50 per ton to carry lumber shorter distances at no greater cost.[127] The typical regulatory agency would view such a competitive price response as an unjust discrimination against R' and would insist that R's coal rates include a proportional share of the road's fixed costs.[128] In defense of the agency's view, one might argue that if R' has no monopoly markets to which to allocate a disproportionate share of its fixed costs, it is being undersold only because R has the advantage of monopoly power in another market. But that is a superficial analysis. A firm

[125]*See, e.g.*, R. Caves, Air Transport and Its Regulators: An Industry Study 169–76, 192–231 (1962); C. Fulda, Competition in the Regulated Industries: Transportation 82–87 (1961); L. Keyes, Federal Control of Entry Into Air Transportation (1951); Adams, *The Regulatory Commissions and Small Business*, 24 Law & Contemp. Prob. 147, 150–52 (1959); Nelson, *The Effects of Entry Control in Surface Transport*, in Transportation Economics 381 (Nat'l Bureau Econ. Research 1965).

[126]Also a form of regulation for which a coherent economic rationale is difficult to supply. *See* text accompanying note 82 *supra*.

[127]*See* text accompanying note 46 *supra*.

[128]For a recent example see American Commercial Lines v. Louisville & N.R. Co., 392 U.S. 571 (1968) (the "ingot molds" case).

that can spread its fixed costs over more sales, in however many markets, is more efficient than a firm with a smaller output. That is what economies of scale—the concept that lies at the heart of natural monopoly—means. Adherence to the principle that price must always reflect fully distributed costs, regardless of the demand conditions facing the regulated firm, is probably responsible for a very substantial waste of resources. Because railroads have been forbidden to offer attractive yet remunerative rates that would enable them to put idle capacity to work, a great deal of business has been improperly diverted to motor carriers and barge lines, resulting in a larger total transportation plant than actually required to meet the needs of society.[129]

While pricing by fully distributed costs is inefficient, and probably very seriously so, it is understandable why regulatory agencies are reluctant to abandon such a relatively simple method of rate regulation: The economically sound method does not appear to be administratively feasible. The economic test of a rate's consistency with allocative efficiency is whether it covers the cost of expanding output in order to serve the favored customer, that is, the "incremental" or "marginal" cost. But to embrace incremental-cost pricing as a regulatory standard is to embark on a sea of uncertainties. An example will illustrate one of the several kinds of difficulties involved. Suppose a pipeline company has a 10-inch pipeline between two points. The pipeline is full and demand is growing. The company cannot expand the diameter of the pipeline; it can only install a second pipeline. Should that be a 2-inch or a 10-inch pipeline? Although the latter will have excess capacity initially, it may be less costly in the long run to install the larger pipeline today than to install the smaller one today and a third pipeline in a few years. But construction of the larger pipeline now may not be dictated by efficiency. It is conceivable—although, in view of our earlier discussion of predatory pricing, improbable—that construction of the larger pipeline could have a more sinister motive: to set the stage for well-concealed predatory pricing tactics. The incremental cost of service in a pipeline that has unused capacity is very low. No entrant will be able to meet a price equal to that cost, even though if the pipeline company had built the smaller pipeline (which we will assume would have been the effi-

[129]*See, e.g.,* J. Nelson, Railroad Transportation and Public Policy 346–47 (1959); Peck, *Competitive Policy for Transportation?*, in Perspectives on Antitrust Policy 244, 257, 263–64 (A. Phillips ed. 1965).

cient solution) a subsequent entrant could have competed for later increments of demand. In order to differentiate a spurious incremental cost created by initial overbuilding from a legitimate incremental cost based on an unavoidable discontinuity between capacity and immediate demand, the regulatory agency would have to immerse itself in the details of the company's construction program. But this is an area where the agencies, as we shall see, have exercised only nominal review of corporate decisions and cannot be expected to do much better.[130]

In sum, an agency predisposed to protect the existing sellers will use its power over entry to block the growth of competition. An agency disposed to permit greater competition may adopt a liberal policy toward entry but then fail to hold entrants to the test of survivorship due to inability to determine whether the incumbent firms' pricing responses are predatory or legitimately competitive.

Our point that regulation of rates and entry unjustifiably inhibits competition could be developed at much greater length. But it has been sufficiently made elsewhere; the impact of regulation on competition has been the subject of a number of excellent studies whose unanimous conclusion is that it has been quite harmful.[131] What is

[130]*See* text accompanying notes 138, 185–87 *infra*. Perhaps the difficulty of using marginal cost as the standard of legally permissible pricing would be reduced somewhat by a rule requiring pricing according to fully distributed cost unless the regulated firm is able to prove that a departure from such pricing is justified by competitive need and that its competitive price is not below marginal cost. (I pass by such interesting questions as whether and in what circumstances this should be "long run" or "short run" or "intermediate run" marginal cost and how to differentiate these periods.) Shifting the burden of proof to the regulated company, however, does not really simplify the determination of marginal cost. It simply makes it rather less likely that the firm will be permitted to depart from pricing according to fully distributed cost than if the burden were on the other side. That would be a move away from what I would conceive to be the proper direction in this area—which is toward more freedom in pricing.

[131]*See, e.g.,* R. CAVES, *supra* note 125; L. KEYES, *supra* note 125; J. MEYER, M. PECK, J. STENASON & C. ZWICK, *supra* note 119; J. NELSON, *supra* note 129, at 145–47; Boise, *Experiment in Mercantilism: Minimum Rate Regulation by the Interstate Commerce Commission,* 68 COLUM. L. REV. 599 (1968); Farmer, *The Case for Unregulated Truck Transportation,* 46 J. FARM ECON. 398 (1964); Hilton, *Barriers to Competitive Ratemaking,* 29 I.C.C. PRAC. J. 1083 (1962); Nelson, *supra* note 125; Wilson, *The Effect of Rate Regulation on Resource Allocation in Transportation,* 54 AM. ECON. REV. PAPERS & PROCEEDINGS 160 (1964); Comment, *supra* note 119. It is true that all of these studies involve the transportation industries, where the elements of natural monopoly are most attenuated. But one would expect the same problems to arise in other regulated industries as and when conditions of natural monopoly begin to wane, a process that can be observed today in the communications industry.

insufficiently emphasized is the circularity of the justifications for regulatory control of profits, of entry, and of specific rates. Control of entry strengthens the argument for limiting the overall profits of the regulated firm. By increasing the difficulty of entry, such control raises the price that a rational monopolist can fix without encouraging entry. It enhances, in other words, the firm's ability to extract monopoly profits from consumers. Being partly responsible for monopoly prices, the government cannot easily justify a posture of indifference to monopoly profits. The fact that the provision of a regulated service requires a license from the government underlies the conception of regulated companies as privileged entities,[132] and the correlative notion that it would be intolerable to permit such a firm to use its privileged status to mulct consumers. This view rests on something of a misconception as applied to natural monopoly markets. The natural monopolist owes his ability to extract monopoly profits to the cost conditions of the market, rather than to the licensing power of the government, except as that power may discourage other firms from seeking to supplant him. But that is an important exception. In time the licensing requirement may become the greatest barrier to new entry into a market.

Given profit regulation that is at all effective, the argument for regulating specific rates is strengthened. As discussed earlier, the danger that an unregulated monopolist will sell below cost to eliminate rivals in a competitive market does not appear substantial, since such predatory price discrimination would require that the monopolist forgo present profits in order to achieve a monopoly in the competitive market and then continue to forgo substantial profits in that market in order to repel entry.[133] On the other hand, if the monopolist's overall profits are limited by regulation he need not forgo pres-

---

[132]It is sometimes suggested that what distinguishes public utilities and common carriers from other companies is that the services they provide are vital to the public, or that they have the power of condemnation, or that duly published tariffs have the force of law until revoked. These are make-weight distinctions. Many industries not regulated as to price—such as the drug industry—are equally purveyors of necessities. The power of condemnation has been given to right-of-way companies because of their peculiar susceptibility to being "held up" by the landowner who knows that the railroad or pipeline company cannot go around him without great expense. The legal effect of tariffs is ancillary to the antidiscrimination provisions of regulatory statutes. In sum, the real root of the sense that public utilities are somehow privileged enterprises is that the government limits entry and thereby contributes to the monopoly power of the enterprise.

[133]See text accompanying note 76 supra.

ent profits in order to sell below cost in competitive markets. He can recoup any losses in the second market by raising his other rates, all the while remaining within the overall profit limitation imposed by the regulatory agency.

The fact that a monopolist whose profits are limited by regulation can sell below cost in some markets without impairing his overall profits does not mean that he will do so. What motives might he have for predatory conduct? One might be to maximize sales or growth, either as an end in itself or as a proxy for long-run profit maximization;[134] another, to use more capital.[135] Whether in practice either motive or both would outweigh the considerable dangers of predatory pricing as a business policy[136] is a difficult question. Nonetheless, the case for minimum-rate regulation is stronger if plant expansion is independently profitable, even if the plant's output must be sold below cost, and if any losses in one market can be recouped by raising prices in another, than if neither condition holds. And neither condition will hold unless overall profits are subject to regulatory limitation.

Once minimum-rate regulation is instituted, the case for regulating entry acquires new plausibility. Now there is reason to fear that entrants will not be put to a survivorship test, but will instead be sheltered through invocation of the agency's minimum-rate power. If the agency also uses its authority over rate structure to foster internal subsidies, there will be an additional reason to regulate entry.

Analytically, the circle is easily broken. Regulation of entry is unjustified and should be abandoned.[137] In its absence, regulation of the overall profits of a natural monopolist has, for the reasons discussed earlier, little appeal. Without profit regulation, there is no persuasive case for placing a floor under the monopolist's rates—since the antitrust laws should provide an adequate safeguard

[134]*See* W. BAUMOL, BUSINESS BEHAVIOR, VALUE AND GROWTH 29–52 (rev. ed. 1967); D. LAMBERTON, THE THEORY OF PROFIT 101–02 (1965).

[135]*See* text accompanying note 98 *supra.*

[136]*See* text accompanying note 81 *supra.*

[137]It may be thought that entry must be limited at least at the local level, in order to protect the public from the inconvenience of having a number of companies ripping up the streets to run gas lines, electric lines, telephone cables, etc. But this problem requires no limitation on entry, only that anyone wishing to rip up the streets be required to reimburse the municipality for the cost (including a reasonable estimate for inconvenience) imposed on the municipality and its residents by the activity.

against unfairly low prices—or for otherwise prescribing the structure of his rates.

Under such a scheme of comprehensive nonregulation, there would be natural monopolists but government would accord them no trace of protection against entrants. They would be free to extract monopoly profits—for as long as they could. They would have strong incentives to adopt policies that maximized internal and possibly also allocative efficiency and optimized the rate and direction of technological change. Although competition would be absent or muted, there are neither a priori nor empirical grounds for confident assertion that free enterprise would not function with reasonable effectiveness or that it would cause substantial social injustice. The principal grounds for concern would be internal inefficiency and the closely related problem of dislodging an incompetent management, but we shall see that neither is the kind of problem that regulation has ever seriously attempted to solve or, in all likelihood, ever could solve.

3. *Regulation of corporate expenditures.*

In theory, regulatory agencies have broad authority over the expenditures of a regulated firm. The firm cannot initiate a new service, abandon an old service, or expand its plant without first obtaining a certificate of public convenience and necessity. More sweeping still, when the regulatory agency reviews the firm's test-year costs it can disallow any expenses imprudently incurred and thereby prevent their recoupment in the future. Spacious in conception, these powers are essentially empty in exercise. It is difficult to document so broad a negative assertion, but anyone who has had firsthand experience with regulatory agencies knows that review of cost items is pro forma and approval routine. Regulatory staffs will admit privately that they rubberstamp the construction programs of regulated firms and only rarely question the prudence of their test-year expenses, except perhaps in a rare case in which a competitor or some other interested party raises an objection.[138] Given the limited budgets of

[138]Even then, we find statements like the following in a recent FCC decision approving a fifth transatlantic cable over Comsat's objection: "[W]e do not believe that any useful purpose would be served by going over relative costs . . . ." "[W]e do not feel it necessary to make definitive findings on the relative merits of TAT-5 and present [or future] satellites." "[T]here are difficulties in making comparisons between cable and satellite costs . . . ." American Tel. & Tel. Co., 13 F.C.C.2d 235, 242–43 & n.4

regulatory commissions and their primary emphasis on rate-of-return and rate-structure matters, it seems clear that the regulatory process, at least as presently conducted, cannot oversee or audit the efficiency and progressiveness of corporate operations. If our analysis of the perverse effects of profit regulation on economic performance is correct, this may be a tragic failure.

4. *Control of restrictive practices.*

Regulatory agencies have been quite active in the area of unfair or restrictive competitive practices, sometimes prohibiting practices that in the absence of regulation would violate the antitrust laws or the Federal Trade Commission Act, but often approving them (price-fixing agreements among railroads, for example). The basic question that this branch of regulatory activity raises is why ordinary antitrust rules cannot be applied through the usual institutions (courts, the Department of Justice, the Federal Trade Commission) to natural monopoly as to other industries. There is no antithesis between antitrust policy, intelligently conceived, and the achievement of efficient performance under conditions of natural monopoly; efficiency is (or should be) the paramount goal of antitrust.[139] The existence of a natural monopoly would be a proper defense to a monopolization suit,[140] and it should also, as argued earlier,[141] be a good defense to a merger suit under the Clayton Act. It would not be a defense to a charge of unlawful price fixing, but neither should it be, in light of our conclusion that the fear that under conditions of natural monopoly price competition will be wasteful is unfounded.[142] One can, of course, question whether the institutions that enforce the an-

---

(1968). Of course, in exceptional cases agencies do disallow expense items or insist on changes in operating procedures. *See, e.g.,* Ogden Tel. Co., 50 P.U.R.3d 219 (N.Y. Pub. Serv. Comm. 1963); North Missouri Tel. Co., 49 P.U.R.3d 313 (Mo. Pub. Serv. Comm. 1963); C. RUGGLES, PROBLEMS IN PUBLIC UTILITY ECONOMICS AND MANAGEMENT 646–69 (2d ed. 1938). However, the general impression of students of the regulatory process conforms to mine: Regulators do very little to police corporate expenditures. *See, e.g.,* E. CLEMENS, ECONOMICS AND PUBLIC UTILITIES 127–31 (1950); H. KOONTZ & R. GABEL, PUBLIC CONTROL OF ECONOMIC ENTERPRISE 257–59 (1956); C. WILCOX, PUBLIC POLICIES TOWARD BUSINESS 560–62, 616 (3d ed. 1966).

[139]*See* C. KAYSEN & D. TURNER, ANTITRUST POLICY 45 (1959).

[140]*See* United States v. Aluminum Co. of America, 148 F.2d 416, 429–30 (2d Cir. 1945) (dictum); United States v. United Shoe Machinery Corp., 110 F. Supp. 295, 343 n.1 (D. Mass. 1953) (dictum), *aff'd mem.,* 347 U.S. 521 (1954).

[141]*See* text accompanying notes 74–75 *supra.*

[142]*See* text preceding note 70 *supra.*

titrust laws would be sufficiently sensitive to the special economic conditions of industries that have strong natural monopoly features. However, the record of those institutions in dealing intelligently with restrictive practices in a wide variety of industry settings seems at least as good as that of the regulatory agencies in dealing with the same practices in the regulated industries.

C. Regulation—The Balance Sheet

Summarizing the discussion to this point, there are different degrees of justification for the various regulatory controls, but in no case do the benefits clearly outweigh the costs. There is no persuasive case for the regulation of specific rates in, or of entry into, natural monopoly markets; yet these have been important areas of regulatory activity, whose principal result has been to promote inefficient pricing and to create unjustified barriers to entry and competition. There is a stronger case for reviewing the planning and expenditures of a natural monopolist, especially if he is not assumed to be exclusively concerned with maximizing short-run profits; but the regulatory agencies have been largely inactive in this area. We registered our concern that an inefficient management might retain control of a monopolistic firm longer than under competition; here is another area where the agencies have been practically helpless. The outcome of the FCC's investigation of Western Union is revealing in this connection. The investigation resulted in a staff report that advised the company to reduce telegram prices selectively in order to recapture business from the telephone companies.[143] Western Union's management disagreed with the staff's diagnosis. They claimed, and still claim, that to reduce telegram rates would be to throw good money after bad. They have not implemented the staff's recommendation—but they have persuaded the Commission to authorize further rate increases.[144]

The case for limiting a natural monopolist's profits turns out, on careful examination, to be weaker than generally assumed. Moreover, either the cure may be worth little because regulatory agencies cannot clamp an effective lid on monopoly profits, or it may be worse than the disease. If at all effective, a ceiling on profits may have seri-

---

[143]See REPORT OF THE TELEPHONE AND TELEGRAPH COMMITTEES OF THE FEDERAL COMMUNICATIONS COMMISSION IN THE DOMESTIC TELEGRAPH INVESTIGATION, FCC Docket No. 14650 (Apr. 29, 1966); Trebing, *Plight of the Telegraph Service*, M.S.U. BUS. TOPICS, Summer 1967, at 43.

[144]See, e.g., Western Union Tel. Co., 12 F.C.C.2d 980 (1968).

ous disincentive effects. It may impair the motivation to minimize costs, to innovate, and to probe for areas of elastic demand. It may encourage a variety of wasteful expenditures. It may reduce the penalty to the firm of predatory and other inefficient pricing policies. Although impossible to measure from present data, these effects provide a forceful answer not only to the efficiency but to the distributive arguments for profit regulation, even if the injustice and undesirability of transferring income from consumers to investors be fully conceded. There are a number of methods that can be employed to divide up the wealth pie so as to favor some groups over others. Except as a last resort, society seems ill advised to use a method that in the process of slicing up the pie may very well make it smaller. Most consumers would rather pay $1 for a long-distance call, 20 cents of which represented a monopoly profit for the telephone company, than $1.10, all of which was cost. If in pursuit of distributive equality society impairs the conditions that would encourage natural monopolists to minimize costs, to innovate, and to price efficiently, it may harm the intended beneficiary of its efforts— the consumer—more than it helps him. No one knows what the actual magnitudes are here; it is a sufficient indictment that we lack any reason to be confident that efforts to limit the profits of natural monopolists, to the extent that they are successful, result in a net social gain.

A proper cost-benefit analysis of regulation must include on the cost side not only the undesirable side effects of regulation but also its administrative costs to both government and industry. The combined budgets of all state and federal regulatory agencies amounted to some $150 million in 1966.[145] In addition, the state and federal judiciaries devote a substantial portion of their time to regulatory cases. Quantification of these opportunity costs is impossible. How, for example, might one value the benefits to the nation of relieving the Justices of the Supreme Court from a burdensome addition to

---

[145]This figure is computed from the 1967 annual reports of the Federal Power Commission, Federal Communications Commission, Interstate Commerce Commission, Federal Maritime Commission, and Civil Aeronautics Board, and in the case of the state regulatory agencies from SUBCOMM. ON INTERGOVERNMENTAL RELATIONS OF THE SENATE COMM. ON GOVERNMENT OPERATIONS, STATE UTILITY COMMISSIONS—SUMMARY AND TABULATION OF INFORMATION SUBMITTED BY THE COMMISSIONS, S. DOC. No. 56, 90th Cong., 1st Sess. 22–23 (1967).

their workload[146] and thereby freeing their time and energies for the more important work of the Court?

One observer has estimated that industry's expenditures on regulatory affairs ("counterregulation," so to speak) are 2.5 to 5 times those of the agencies.[147] This range seems, if anything, too low. For one thing, it ignores the expenses incurred by industry in judicial proceedings arising out of regulatory action. More broadly, regulatory agencies stand in much the same relation to regulated firms as courts to litigants: They sit in judgment on records and submissions prepared by the private parties that appear before them. And far greater expenses are incurred in preparing cases than in judging them. If we assume (conservatively, it seems to me) that industry spends 5 times what the agencies spend on regulation, and if we ignore the opportunity costs of judges, economists, law professors, and others who devote working time to regulation, the administrative cost of regulation is still almost $1 billion annually. The other social costs of regulation that we have discussed may be far greater.[148] And for the reasons noted earlier there is no reason to believe that the benefits of regulation, if they could be quantified, would be found to exceed its direct and indirect costs.

D. *The Forces That Have Shaped the Regulatory Process*

Why, considering its doubtful merits, did regulation develop in the first place? Why has it persisted? Why is it today almost universally accepted as fundamentally worthwhile? An adequate answer to these questions would require a wide-ranging inquiry into the political, economic, intellectual, and educational history and character of America. I shall not attempt such an inquiry, but I would like to

[146] Assuming that the length of an opinion is a rough index to the amount of time the Justices devote to a case, regulation occupied by my calculation approximately $1/8$ of their time in the last Term of Court.

[147] Gerwig, *Natural Gas Production: A Study of Costs of Regulation,* 5 J. LAW & ECON. 69, 86 (1962).

[148] *Cf. id.* at 74. Gerwig's study found that certain direct and indirect costs of regulation of natural-gas producers by the FPC amounted to 7 percent of the base price of natural gas. *Id.* at 91. Projecting this result to the regulated industries as a whole would produce a total cost of regulation of $5 billion a year. (In 1967 the gross product of the regulated sector—transportation, communications, electric, gas, and sanitary services—was $68 billion. Computed from U.S. Dep't of Commerce, Office of Business Economics, 48 SURVEY OF CURRENT BUSINESS, Apr. 1968, at 8.) Since, however, the regulation of gas producers presents special characteristics, it is doubtful whether such a projection is particularly meaningful.

suggest very briefly four factors that seem to provide the essential explanation. They are the reaction, or perhaps overreaction, to laissez faire that characterized the late 19th and early 20th centuries; the businessman's innate distaste for too vigorous competition; the general absence of interdisciplinary training or study in public policy questions; and the institutional limitations of public administration.

Until comparatively recent times, government regulation of prices and other elements of business behavior had been the rule.[149] But beginning in the 18th century, and with increasing momentum, notions of "laissez faire"—of leaving the function of determining price and output to the market—gained ascendancy and many existing restrictions were removed.[150] In the last quarter of the 19th century a powerful reaction set in.[151] I shall not pause to consider whether the complaints of farmers against railroads were justified, or whether the machinations of robber barons really were responsible for depressions. Important segments of opinion believed so and generalized their distaste for the real or supposed failings of an enterprise economy into a broad distrust of the free market.[152] A natural focus of distrust was the monopoly supplier of an essential service, for there the opportunity for abuse was seemingly the greatest.[153] In an era when the modern theory of the firm was undeveloped, it was also natural that important but subtle distinctions, for example between supra-competitive profits as a pure economic rent and as an incentive for efficient and progressive operation, were generally overlooked.[154]

[149]*See, e.g.,* J. HURST, LAW AND THE CONDITIONS OF FREEDOM IN THE NINETEENTH-CENTURY UNITED STATES 38 (1956); Adler, *Business Jurisprudence,* 28 HARV. L. REV. 135 (1914).

[150]*See, e.g.,* 1 L. LYON, M. WATKINS & V. ABRAMSON, GOVERNMENT AND ECONOMIC LIFE 14–17, 23 (1939); A. SHONFIELD, MODERN CAPITALISM: THE CHANGING BALANCE OF PUBLIC AND PRIVATE POWER 304–06 (1965); *cf.* Crouch, *Laissez-Faire in Nineteenth Century Britain: Myth or Reality?,* 35 MANCHESTER SCHOOL ECON. & SOCIAL STUDIES 199 (1967).

[151]Actually, the growth of regulation at the state level had begun somewhat earlier. *See* L. HARTZ, ECONOMIC POLICY AND DEMOCRATIC THOUGHT: PENNSYLVANIA, 1776–1860 (1948); Hunter, *The Early Regulation of Public Service Corporations,* 7 AM. ECON. REV. 569 (1917).

[152]For the spirit of the times see, *e.g.,* ROOSEVELT, WILSON AND THE TRUSTS (E. Rozwenc ed. 1950); A. JOHNSON, THE DEVELOPMENT OF AMERICAN PETROLEUM PIPELINES—A STUDY IN PRIVATE ENTERPRISE AND PUBLIC POLICY, 1862–1906 (1956).

[153]The history of the regulatory movement is described in detail in M. FAINSOD, L. GORDON & J. PALAMOUNTAIN, GOVERNMENT AND THE AMERICAN ECONOMY 239–407 (3d ed. 1959); M. GLAESER, PUBLIC UTILITIES IN AMERICAN CAPITALISM 14–154 (1957); M. GLAESER, OUTLINES OF PUBLIC UTILITY ECONOMICS 195–310 (1927).

[154]Though not completely. *See, e.g.,* C. MORGAN, REGULATION AND THE MANAGEMENT OF PUBLIC UTILITIES (1923); I. BUSSING, PUBLIC UTILITY REGULATION AND THE SO-CALLED SLIDING SCALE (1936).

Nor is it surprising that disenchantment with market forces was matched with what now appears to have been an exaggerated faith in the independence and expertise of government administrators.[155] Pessimism about free enterprise and optimism about government regulation reached their peak during the New Deal era. The Great Depression seemed to many to reveal the bankruptcy of the market as an economic regulator, and the scope of regulation was once more broadened.[156] There was an element of *non sequitur* here. It was primarily the inadequacy of fiscal, monetary, and welfare policy that made the depression so painful and so prolonged. But that was not clearly perceived.

The regulatory movement was fortunate in the stature of the men who enlisted in its support—men such as Wilson, Brandeis, and Frankfurter. It also won the support of the more enlightened business leaders, such as Theodore N. Vail of the Bell System, who realized that the alternative to regulation might be government expropriation.[157] The economics profession failed, by and large, to subject the weak premises of the regulatory process to critical scrutiny.[158] Its necessity and basic wisdom became a firmly embedded element of our intellectual heritage—the heritage of today's regulators and their staffs.

It is important to note, however, that the reformers and their natural allies (such as farmers and small merchants) might never have succeeded in imposing regulatory controls had not many carriers and utilities perceived reasons of self-interest to welcome them. I alluded to the fact that some farsighted business leaders saw regulation as the only alternative to government expropriation. Others saw it as protection against competition. It is entirely natural that businessmen should seek ways to eliminate competition, for competition increases risk and reduces profit. In the late 19th century the railroads in this country attempted to eliminate price competition by

[155]The classic paean to administration is J. LANDIS, THE ADMINISTRATIVE PROCESS (1938).

[156]E. HAWLEY, THE NEW DEAL AND THE PROBLEM OF MONOPOLY (1966), contains a good discussion of New Deal economic policies and measures. For an example of the profound mistrust of competition that characterized the period and that played a significant part in the extension of regulation to naturally competitive industries such as trucking, barges, and airlines see REGULATION OF TRANSPORTATION AGENCIES—REPORT OF FEDERAL COORDINATOR OF TRANSPORTATION AGENCIES, S. Doc. No. 152, 73d Cong., 2d Sess. (1934).

[157]*See* P. GARFIELD & W. LOVEJOY, PUBLIC UTILITY ECONOMICS 449 (1964).

[158]*See, e.g.,* 2 F. FAIRCHILD, E. FURNISS & S. BUCK, ELEMENTARY ECONOMICS 23–26 (1926).

forming cartels, but the cartel agreements kept breaking down.[159] Foreseeing—correctly as it turned out[160]—that regulation would dampen price competition by requiring them to adhere to published tariff rates and by limiting discrimination, the railroads threw their weight behind the proposals for an Interstate Commerce Act.[161] The pattern has recurred repeatedly in the history of regulation.[162] The reader should also recall the earlier discussion of how regulation creates barriers to entry, protecting the market positions of regulated firms. The short of it is that regulated firms, perhaps more than their customers, have a powerful economic interest in the continuation of regulation.

In considering why a realistic appraisal of the costs and benefits of regulation has been slow to develop, the character of education in the disciplines relating to public-policy questions, and the patterns of research that have resulted, should not be overlooked. Public utility regulation is not encompassed by any single discipline. Economics is clearly important, I would say fundamental; but law and political science are also highly relevant. Failure to integrate the three disciplines has hampered useful work in the field.

I mean no criticism of economists, who have contributed some splendid studies of regulation, in pointing out that they are not, and do not claim to be, experts on legal procedures and institutions. An economist can tell you what in principle the regulatory process should require of firms in order to assure efficient performance, but not whether the desired controls are practical, given the limitations of institutions. Somewhat prone to assume that government can actually compel whatever business conduct is deemed desirable as a matter of economic theory, many economists, in comparing market to administrative solutions of monopoly problems, tend to underrate the often intractable difficulties of administration.[163] We shall see this quite clearly when we discuss economists' proposals for reform of the regulatory process.

---

[159]See P. MacAvoy, The Economic Effects of Regulation: The Trunk-Line Railroad Cartels and the Interstate Commerce Commission Before 1900 passim (1965).

[160]See id. at 195.

[161]See Hilton, The Consistency of the Interstate Commerce Act, 9 J. Law & Econ. 87, 105 (1966), and studies cited therein.

[162]See sources cited in note 2 supra.

[163]The point has been very well made by an economist. Coase, The Regulated Industries—Discussion, 54 Am. Econ. Rev. Papers & Proceedings 196 (1964).

Political scientists have made valuable contributions to a more realistic understanding of the regulatory process, and in particular the degree to which the process is involved with politics.[164] Again, however, the perspective is an incomplete one. Political scientists are not in general interested in the substantive economic ends of regulation. And neither political scientists nor economists can feel entirely at home with the highly legalistic form of regulation—the pervasive emphasis on legal rights and remedies.

Lawyers in fact dominate the regulatory process. Commissioners and leading staff members are drawn almost wholly from their ranks. Most legislators are lawyers and so are most of the representatives of the regulated firms who appear before the agencies, and all of the judges who review regulatory action. A lawyer's training and experience are indispensable to the practical implementation of social policy. What is too readily assumed is that lawyers are also expert in the underlying policies themselves, a view that lawyers, who are among the most facile of "generalists," eagerly promote. Unhappily, the overwhelming majority of lawyers involved with regulation are largely ignorant of the principles of economics. Most lawyers have had undergraduate economics courses, yet my experience (and others') has been that such courses generally fail to make a lasting impression so far as aiding later insight into regulatory problems is concerned,[165] partly, perhaps, because the treatment of regulated industries in economics textbooks tends to be bland and uncritical.[166] Most law schools do little to remedy this deficiency. A law student's exposure to the regulated industries is normally limited to the administrative-law class, which deals with procedural questions, not with economic policies.[167] What law schools principally instill in

[164]*See* note 103 *supra.*

[165]The economics profession is quite aware of the general problem. *See, e.g.,* Bach, *The Efficiency of Education in Economics,* 5 W. ECON. J. 1 (1966).

[166]*See, e.g.,* P. SAMUELSON, ECONOMICS: AN INTRODUCTORY ANALYSIS 466–82, 495–97 (7th ed. 1967). This is also true of textbooks specifically devoted to regulation. *See, e.g.,* C. PHILLIPS, THE ECONOMICS OF REGULATION (1965). Some of the texts on industrial organization contain good discussions of regulation. *See* J. BAIN, INDUSTRIAL ORGANIZATION 633–45 (2d ed. 1968); L. WEISS, ECONOMICS AND AMERICAN INDUSTRY 224–69 (1962).

[167]Few law schools offer regulated-industries courses at all, let alone courses with a substantial economics content. And the law professor who wants to infuse some elementary economics into such a course will not find a casebook that meets his need. The best casebook, in my judgment, is W. JONES, CASES AND MATERIALS ON REGULATED INDUSTRIES (1967). While Professor Jones' economic sophistication is apparent from the questions he has put after each block of materials, the book contains no systematic pre-

their students is sensitivity to the formal processes of the law and to considerations of fairness and equity, emphases that go far to explain the continuing preoccupation of both practicing lawyers and legal scholars with the procedural and distributional questions in the regulatory field—such as how much of the pie should investors get and how much consumers. Issues as or more important to the welfare of society—issues of economic efficiency in the broadest sense of that term—are usually ignored because they are the province of a different discipline. In this fashion, the compartmentalization of scholarly and professional interest in regulatory problems has retarded an adequate understanding of those problems.

Perhaps the most important factor supporting the continuation of public utility regulation without reference to its actual social utility is its institutional character.[168] Because regulatory commissions are of necessity intimately involved in the affairs of a particular industry, the regulators and their staffs are exposed to strong interest-group pressures. Their susceptibility to pressures that may distort economically sound judgments is enhanced by the tradition of regarding regulatory commissions as "arms of the legislature," where interest-group pressures naturally play a vitally important role. To the extent that regulation is bent by these pressures to confer private benefits that a free market would withhold, such as service below cost to some consumers or legal protections against entry, it gives rise to vested economic interests that will oppose the removal of regulatory controls regardless of broader welfare considerations.

What is insufficiently emphasized is that within government itself there are vested interests in the continuation of regulation. Regulation is for the average regulator (especially if he is a member of the staff rather than one of the commissioners) his livelihood, and for the dedicated regulator his mission and purpose in life. There are many frustrations to government service, and the pecuniary rewards are not adequate compensation for them. Regulators tend, in consequence, to be of two types. One consists of individuals unable to obtain "better" employment as judged by the conventional criteria of

sentation of the economic concepts relevant to an evaluation of the regulatory process, and few excerpts from or even references to the economic literature. It assumes that the instructor is fully conversant with the economic principles relevant to regulation, an assumption that in most cases is probably unwarranted.

[168]Jaffe, *The Effective Limits of the Administrative Process: A Reevaluation*, 67 HARV. L. REV. 1105 (1954), is an excellent treatment of this subject.

success; they would suffer in their pocketbooks if the activities of regulatory agencies were drastically curtailed. The other and more interesting consists of individuals who identify with the purposes of the regulatory agency and, more broadly, with the purposes of regulation. I can attest from personal experience that such individuals are often highly motivated and competent. Their strength, however, is also their weakness. Commitment to regulation blends insensibly into exaggerated faith in the effectiveness of regulation, and what is especially disquieting about such a faith is that its frequent corollary is a distrust of the market even in instances where reliance on market forces would manifestly be a superior alternative to continuing or extending regulatory controls. Those whose business it is to control economic forces have difficulty perceiving the virtues of free markets. Also conspicuous is the disposition of conscientious regulatory personnel to polarize the issues and personalize the disputants before the agency, to translate impersonal and rarely simple economic questions into a war between good and evil[169]—a displacement of emphasis that impedes a rational examination of the monopoly problem and may help to perpetuate regulation beyond its useful life.

III. Proposals for Reform of the Regulatory Process

I suggested earlier that the social gain from public utility and common carrier regulation is quite possibly negative. It would be too abrupt, however, to conclude from this that regulation should be abandoned. The possibilities for constructive reform must first be assessed.

A. *Determining the True Cost of Equity Capital*

The regulatory process cannot function effectively according to its own criteria—cannot eliminate monopoly profits—unless the true cost of equity capital can be ascertained. Otherwise the fair-return component in the cost of service becomes a convenient loophole. As noted earlier, the conventional methods of determining fair return are clearly inadequate. Awareness of this fact has prompted a number of recent proposals for reform. The essence of these proposals is to tie the allowed return on equity to the actual expectations and requirements of investors, as manifested by their behavior in the mar-

---

[169]*Cf.* G. HENDERSON, THE FEDERAL TRADE COMMISSION 341 (1924).

ket in which equity capital is obtained—the stock market. A recent note in the *Stanford Law Review* delineates such a proposal.[170] While not the most fully elaborated of these proposals,[171] it sufficiently illustrates the principle and its relative simplicity facilitates exposition.

The method proposed in the note is to limit the allowed return on equity capital to the ratio between the earnings per share of the firm's equity stock and the market price of the share (averaged over a reasonable period). Suppose, for example, that the common stock of regulated firm *A* is selling at $50 per share; the total market price of the outstanding shares is $20 million; and the annual earnings per share (based on an allowed return of 9 percent of the $13 million equity component of the firm's rate base) is $3, 6 percent of the market price. Under the proposal, the allowed rate of return would be reduced to 6 percent. Applied to *A*'s rate base—which is significantly smaller than the aggregate market value of its stock—a 6 percent rate of return yields earnings of only $2 per share. This is well below the 6 percent of market price currently demanded by the market and will cause the market price of *A* to drop. As it drops, the allowed rate of return will be readjusted upward, until eventually an equilibrium is reached. At that point, it is said, the regulatory agency is allowing the exact rate of return that the market demands, and profit and cost of capital are equated.

The method achieves certainty in the determination of the cost of equity capital, but at the considerable price of drastically impairing the regulated firm's incentive to improve performance. Any such improvement would normally be reflected in a rise in the market value of the stock. But under the earnings-price method any rise in price automatically triggers a cut in earnings. There is a built-in penalty for success. From the investor's standpoint, successful operation is self-defeating. For what the method does in realistic as opposed to formal terms is not to ascertain the cost of equity capital but to change the capital structure of regulated firms. Because the allowed earnings of the firm are keyed directly to the market price of the stock, falling as

---

[170]Note, *An Earnings-Price Approach to Fair Rate of Return in Regulated Industries*, 20 STAN. L. REV. 287 (1968). To similar effect see E. CLEMENS, ECONOMICS AND PUBLIC UTILITIES 241–43 (1950).

[171]A much more elaborate approach, based, however, on the same basic principle—investor expectations as revealed by stock-price fluctuations—is proposed in Testimony of Myron J. Gordon, FCC Docket 16258, FCC Staff Exhibit No. 17 (1966) (A.T.&T. rate inquiry).

the price of the stock in the market rises and rising as the market price falls, the inevitable tendency is to stabilize price and earnings. That is a radical departure from normal corporate practice, where profits are not directly dependent on stock market values and are not reduced by management or government merely because the market price is rising. Functionally, the difference between a stock whose market gyrations are contained by manipulation of profit levels and a stock whose market value has no feedback effect on the firm's earnings is the difference between a bond (constant price and return, regardless of the profit fluctuations of the firm) and common stock as ordinarily conceived, where price fluctuates freely with changes in the firm's profit picture.

Under the earnings-price approach, then, regulated firms are in effect compelled to resort to revenue bonds to satisfy any capital needs that cannot be satisfied in the ordinary bond market. They cannot lure investors with a promise of greater profits in the future, for the investors know that if those profits materialize and cause the price of the stock to rise, profits will promptly be reduced, causing the stock price to plummet. Beneath all this is the unstated assumption that the capital structure of regulated firms should be composed entirely of debt, presumably because such firms are sufficiently low risk to be comparable to the public authorities that rely entirely on unsecured bond financing to satisfy their capital requirements.[172] But to state the matter thus is to pose the question of incentives most starkly. If the "owners" of the enterprise are in effect creditors limited to a fixed return, where is the incentive to improve efficiency? The managers are truly autonomous in these circumstances and profit maximization ceases to be a rational or meaningful strategy. How, then, are proper incentives to be created? Should the managers receive any profits that remain (due, say, to regulatory lag) after the bondholders receive their fixed return, or perhaps a percentage of the profits with the rest being taxed away by the Government? Or should they be given bonuses for demonstrated improvements in efficiency? The first option is appealing but hardly a complete answer since if the general trend of costs is upward there may be no opportunity to profit from regulatory lag; one would also be concerned about the removal of

---

[172]Unless the firm is wholly risk free, however, the absence of a cushion of equity stock will cause an increase in the interest rate that the firm must pay for bond financing. *See* Baumol & Malkiel, *The Firm's Optimal Debt-Equity Combination and the Cost of Capital,* 81 Q.J. ECON. 547 (1967).

whatever check the capital market and the possibility of a takeover may exert on managerial behavior. The second suggestion, bonuses for demonstrated efficiency, involves all the difficulties that will be considered below in discussing incentive methods of regulation.

The earnings-price method, in attempting to avoid the ambiguities and circularities of the comparable-earnings method,[173] raises difficult problems of its own.[174] The goal of accurately controlling a monopolist's profits without destroying his incentives to efficiency remains elusive. One could easily extend the analysis to show that the other loopholes of profit regulation, such as the difficulty of allocating joint costs, are equally resistant to practical solution.

B. *Incentive Regulation*

If, aside from sheer ineffectiveness, the major problem with regulatory limitation of profits is, as I would argue, its pernicious effects on business incentives, why is not the answer for regulatory agencies explicitly to permit the regulated firm to retain those profits that represent not the exploitation of its monopoly position but superior efficiency? Supporters of this perennial proposal[175] have unfortunately been unable to dispel the considerable doubts concerning the practicability of its implementation. The heart of the problem is that good management is a concept stubbornly resistant to precise or quantitative measurement. To be sure, there are some widely accepted principles of good management that relate to cost control, employee incentives, corporate organization, and the like; and regulatory agencies easily could, and perhaps should, insist that regulated firms formally adopt such principles and procedures. But de-

---

[173]*See* text accompanying note 90 *supra.*

[174]For additional problems see Ross, *Comments on the Earnings-Price Note,* 21 STAN. L. REV. 644 (1969).

[175]For recent examples see Klevoric, *The Graduated Fair Return: A Regulatory Proposal,* 56 AM. ECON. REV. 477 (1966); Trebing, *Toward an Incentive System of Regulation,* 72 PUB. UTIL. FORT., July 18, 1963, at 22. Such proposals have an ancient lineage. For an excellent analysis, made in 1923, of methods of incentive regulation see C. MORGAN, *supra* note 154; and for an even earlier proposal for incentive regulation see R. WHITTEN, REGULATION OF PUBLIC SERVICE CORPORATIONS IN GREAT BRITAIN 227–31 (1914). The persistent failure of these proposals to win acceptance, *see* Trebing, *supra* at 28, may indicate something about their practicality. Klevoric's recent proposal, for example, is quite similar to the old "sliding scale" method, which never achieved widespread acceptance in this country. *See* I. BUSSING, *supra* note 154; M. GLAESER, *supra* note 153, at 299–304. The history of incentive regulation, and some of the problems, are discussed in Trebing, *supra.*

ciding whether those principles have been intelligently applied—whether the firm is in fact efficient and well managed—presents difficult problems. The only test that seems reasonably satisfactory is that provided by competition. Sellers in the same market face very similar conditions of cost and demand. If some obtain greater profits than others, presumably it is the quality of management that made the difference.[176]

It is possible, in short, to determine the relative efficiency of similarly situated firms by comparing their business success; it is impossible, or at least hopelessly subjective, to judge a firm's efficiency in the abstract. This, it seems to me, rules out the application of an efficiency standard to determine permitted profit in the case of regulated firms that are unique, notably the Bell System. There is no yardstick against which to evaluate the performance of the Bell System's managers—no remotely comparable firm.

The opportunities for comparison are better in some regulated industries. For example, there are a number of electrical utilities, and academic economists have conducted studies to measure their comparative efficiency.[177] The difficulty that besets such studies is that, unlike competitors, regional or local monopolists do not sell in the same market and consequently do not face the same conditions of cost and demand; the cost differences among them, therefore, cannot be assumed to be the result of differences in managerial competence or foresight. By performing multiple-regression analyses, economists can attempt to factor out the other differential factors and isolate the effects of differences in managerial efficiency; but the data are rarely sufficient to warrant confident conclusions.[178]

---

[176]At least, this should be true for profit differences that have persisted for a sufficient period to cancel out the effects of sheer luck.

[177]See Iulo, *Problems in the Definition and Measurement of Superior Performance*, in PERFORMANCE UNDER REGULATION 3 (H. Trebing ed. 1968); his earlier studies, ELECTRIC UTILITIES—COSTS AND PERFORMANCE (1961), and *The Relative Performance of Individual Electric Utilities*, 38 LAND ECON. 315 (1962); Dodge, *Productivity Measures and Performance Evaluation*, in PERFORMANCE UNDER REGULATION, *supra* at 20; *cf.* Gordon, *Airline Costs and Managerial Efficiency*, in TRANSPORTATION ECONOMICS 61 (Nat'l Bureau Econ. Research 1965). Comparisons of utility performance are no new thing either. *See* C. MORGAN, *supra* note 154, at 24–59.

[178]Thus, Professor Iulo has cautioned against the direct use of his results in regulatory proceedings: "Regulatory application of these procedures, however, would require the examination and evaluation of the unique policies of individual utilities before reaching a final determination as to their relative efficiency." Iulo, *The Relative Performance of Individual Electric Utilities*, 38 LAND ECON. 315, 325 (1962).

It is possible to conceive of vast improvements in the quality and quantity of the data gathered and in the refinement of the mathematical tools for manipulating the data. But anyone who believes that a fruitful direction for forward movement in regulation is toward increasing the amount of the data and the sophistication of the conceptual apparatus used in arriving at regulatory judgments is ignoring the lesson of experience. The movement in the closely related area of antitrust and trade regulation has been in the opposite direction: from broad-ranging inquiries into industry and company performance to rather simple rules of thumb that attach a presumption (often irrebuttable) of illegality to one or a few relatively straightforward elements of business conduct or market structure, such as the existence of an agreement to fix prices or of a high degree of concentration in the relevant market, without attempting to inquire or indeed permitting inquiry as to whether suboptimal performance did or would result.[179] Indeed, I believe it fair to say that performance tests are almost completely discredited as standards of antitrust illegality. Closer to home, the movement from replacement cost to original cost as the basis for determining rate base is in part a product of a similar concern with the enormous practical burdens that the former method places on agency and reviewing court.[180] What these developments reflect (and what economists perhaps tend to overlook) are the institutional limitations of judicial and administrative processes. For reasons that would take us too far afield to explore here, legal proceedings simply are not well adapted to sifting complex economic data and arriving at sound judgments on sophisticated economic questions. They are not a good vehicle for resolving the conflicting results of multiple-regression analyses.

I should mention two further complicating factors. First, efforts to rank managers by efficiency are likely to produce bitter wrangling

[179]*See, e.g.,* United States v. Philadelphia Nat'l Bank, 374 U.S. 321, 362 (1963); Northern Pac. Ry. v. United States, 356 U.S. 1, 5 (1957); C. KAYSEN & D. TURNER, ANTITRUST POLICY 52–56 (1959); E. MASON, ECONOMIC CONCENTRATION AND THE MONOPOLY PROBLEM 392–98 (1957); Bok, *Section 7 of the Clayton Act and the Merging of Law and Economics,* 74 HARV. L. REV. 226 (1960); Brewster, *Enforceable Competition: Unruly Reason or Unreasonable Rules?*, 46 AM. ECON. REV. PAPERS & PROCEEDINGS 482 (1956); Elman, *The National Issue,* in THE IMPACT OF ANTI-TRUST ON ECONOMIC GROWTH—THIRD CONFERENCE ON ANTITRUST IN AN EXPANDING ECONOMY 36, 39–40 (Nat'l Ind. Conf. Bd. 1964).

[180]*See* FPC v. Hope Natural Gas Co., 320 U.S. 591 (1944); Missouri *ex rel.* Southwestern Bell Tel. Co. v. Public Serv. Comm., 262 U.S. 276, 289–90 (1923) (concurring opinion, Brandeis, J.); F. WELCH, CASES AND TEXT ON PUBLIC UTILITY REGULATION 307 (rev. ed. 1968).

simply because a manager will intensely resent being stigmatized by a government agency as an inferior business executive. Second, the concept that there are "management prerogatives" with which government should not tamper lest it sap business initiative retains sufficient force to place a heavy burden upon the agency of demonstrating credibly that one firm has higher costs than another selling in a second market because of differences in efficiency rather than differences in circumstance. In sum, it is a long way from academic studies, however excellent, to a government order that utility X may earn only 6 percent of equity while Y may earn 8 because Y is more efficient. One would anticipate acrimonious, protracted, costly, and ultimately inconclusive litigation over the question why X's costs were higher.[181]

Some observers have proposed "automatic" methods of incentive regulation designed to avoid involving the regulatory agency in explicit appraisals of the firm's efficiency. A recent proposal by William Baumol illustrates the nature of the approach.[182] He suggests a variant of regulatory lag under which (1) at intervals the regulatory agency would fix overall rate requirements at a level that would just return the actual cost of service (including cost of capital) of the regulated firm and (2) during the interim periods the firm would be forbidden to raise its rates. Thus, at each interval, the firm would have no supracompetitive profits. In order to avoid losses it would have to keep its costs from rising, since it could not raise its rates. In order to obtain profits it would have to reduce its costs. These cost reductions would in turn establish a new plateau, and (much as under competition) the firm would have to better its performance in the next period in order to obtain additional profits.[183]

[181]The same difficulties attend Oliver Williamson's suggestion, in his as yet unpublished paper, Administrative Decision-Making and Pricing: Externality Analysis and Regulatory Design, that agencies hire management-consultant firms to do efficiency audits on the regulatees. New York City recently did just that with reference to Consolidated Edison. The management-consultant firm was highly critical of the company, the company replied stormily, and the state public service commission took the company's side. The story is told in a forthcoming book on industrial organization by Frederick M. Scherer of the University of Michigan. It does not augur well for a more general use of the device.

[182]Reasonable Rules for Rate Regulation: Plausible Policies for an Imperfect World, in PRICES: ISSUES IN THEORY, PRACTICE, AND PUBLIC POLICY 108, 114–15 (A. Phillips & O. Williamson eds. 1967).

[183]J. Cross, Incentive Pricing and Utility Regulation (unpublished paper delivered at Brookings Institution Symposium on Rate-Base Regulation, June 7, 1968), proposes

In essence, then, the proposal modifies regulatory lag (whose short-comings as an incentive device were discussed earlier)[184] in two re-spects: (1) the procedure is avowedly, and not merely incidentally, designed to provide a profit incentive to efficient performance—the agency may not order a rate reduction before the end of the specified period—and (2) the regulated firm is not permitted to file for a rate increase during the period just because its costs increase—this to provide "stick" as well as "carrot."

The proposal raises some difficult questions. One is the period within which rate changes are not permitted and monopoly profits can be retained. If the period is a generous one, the monopolist's ability to extract monopoly profits may approach that of an unregu-lated monopolist, especially when we recall the many other loop-holes in profit regulation. If a short period is fixed, the opportunity to obtain monopoly profits (and hence the incentive to reduce costs) may be less than under the existing situation of regulatory lags uncertain in their duration, conceivably so much less as to destroy the incentive feature of the technique. The selection of a period that accommodates the conflicting goals of limiting profits and of al-lowing them as a reward for cost reductions is, to say the least, not easy.

Any fixed, pre-announced period, moreover, carries the danger of distorting the regulated firm's business judgments. The firm will at-tempt to postpone cost reductions until after its next rate plateau is determined in order to capture as much of the savings as possible for its investors. On the other hand, were a flexible or random period employed, the firm, much as under today's regulatory lag, would lack assurance that it could retain a substantial part of any cost sav-ings it was able to generate. But however the period between the reg-

---

a variant method under which the regulated firm would be required to reduce its price by a percentage (such as 50 percent) of any cost reduction occurring after the price is initially fixed. Thus, whereas Baumol allows the firm all the profits it can obtain by cost reduction between rate determinations, Cross would allow it somewhat less. No-tice, though, that the actual profits obtained by the regulated firm would normally ex-ceed the percentage of the cost reduction that it was not required to pass on to the con-sumer—this because an appropriate price reduction to take advantage of a cost reduction will result in a larger profit to the monopolist than if he held price constant, unless demand is totally price inelastic. *See* note 57 *supra*. Something quite like Cross' suggestion was actually used by the Washington, D.C., Public Utilities Commission for many years, with mixed results. *See* Trebing, *supra* note 175, at 28–31.

[184]*See* text accompanying notes 96–97 *supra*.

ulatory rate settings be formulated, the Baumol proposal does not escape the principal drawback of regulatory lag as an incentive method: the danger that *any* substantial curtailment of profit opportunities may impair a monopolist's incentives, especially (and critically) his incentive to innovate.

There is an additional problem with the proposal. If during one of the interim periods costs rise for reasons that reflect no discredit on the firm's management, should it be forced to suffer losses by being forbidden to increase its rates? That seems an incongruous result; under competition, after all, a seller normally does not suffer losses as a result of external cost factors common to his competitors. It is also quite possible—it has been the recent experience of the electric-utility industry—for costs to *fall* as a result of factors external to the regulated firm such as innovations by the manufacturers of electric generators or transmission apparatus. In such a case, to allow a firm to keep the profits that such cost reductions made possible does not reward efficiency; the profits are windfalls. To steer between the shoals of gratuitous punishment and gratuitous reward, the regulatory agency, in applying this supposedly "automatic" incentive method, must factor out any exogenous forces, whether they caused costs to rise or to fall—that, or permit rate increases whenever costs increase, as is the present practice. To require the agency to factor out exogenous forces, however, is to require it to make explicit appraisals of efficiency. Cost trends external to the firm are those outside of the power of management— those that do not vary with managerial efficiency. To factor them out is in effect to decide how efficiently the firm's management is functioning. We are back to efficiency as our regulatory standard.

It is difficult to imagine a rational scheme of incentive regulation that would avoid explicit comparisons of the efficiency of regulated firms. If incentive regulation means nothing more than formally approving the effect of regulatory lag, which enables regulated firms to benefit from lower costs however caused, it does not improve upon the existing system of regulation. Executives of regulated firms today are fully aware that regulatory lag allows them to make and keep profits that exceed the "fair return" fixed by the regulatory agency. Telling them that they may keep these profits (or a portion of them) as a reward for superior efficiency is not only superfluous but misleading, since lower costs may not reflect *their* superior efficiency.

C. *Strengthening Regulatory Capability To Supervise Corporate Expenditures*

One can bypass the question of incentives by focusing on the extensive, but today largely unexercised, powers of regulatory agencies over the expenditures of regulated firms. And even if the problem of incentives were soluble and solved one might still wish to shift the emphasis in regulation toward greater monitoring of regulated firms' internal efficiency, in recognition that internal inefficiency may well be a more serious problem of natural monopoly than monopoly profits.[185] Thus, one might ask, if the agency had the capacity to scrutinize corporate expenditures closely, could it not ensure adequate performance? Should not Congress and the state legislatures be persuaded, therefore, to appropriate the funds necessary to hire enough economists, engineers, management experts, and operations researchers to review major corporate spending decisions in depth? A sufficient answer, I am afraid, is that if regulatory agencies could realistically be expected to develop a practical capability for appraising corporate efficiency, the incentive schemes discussed in the previous subpart might be feasible; they are not feasible because direct efficiency appraisals are not feasible. In addition to the points made earlier, one should note that recruitment of the necessary expert personnel might prove quite difficult. The kinds of skilled analysts necessary to appraise corporate efficiency in the technically complex circumstances of most of the regulated industries are in short supply, and legislatures might rightly feel that their services are more urgently needed in other areas of social concern. Even if the necessary personnel could be obtained, there would be the problem of making "efficiency" a workable regulatory standard. Problems of evidence aside, the concept is hardly crystal-clear, and if one lesson emerges from the history of regulation it is that an agency without a reasonably definite mandate will generally perform very poorly.[186] One also suspects that a searching system of efficiency review would have a deleterious effect on the incentives of the regulated firm. If every important management decision is to be reviewed by the agency, the managers may be tempted to shift to it their managerial responsibility, and never act without the advice of

[185]*See* text accompanying note 54 *supra.*
[186]The classic study is H. FRIENDLY, THE FEDERAL ADMINISTRATIVE AGENCIES: THE NEED FOR BETTER DEFINITION OF STANDARDS (1962).

an agency staff that is neither trained nor accountable for making business judgments.

To illustrate the foregoing points, suppose that the agency's system-design team disagrees with the corporation's as to whether a nuclear or a hydroelectric generating plant should be built, or where, or on what scale. Who will prevail? In a close case, the corporation will. Standards of sound managerial judgment are elusive; and it is, after all, the corporation that must lay its money on the line—the agency's experts are "second guessers." Who *should* prevail? Again, in a close case the corporation should. There are grave dangers in separating power from responsibility—in allowing government officials to decide how private companies should deploy their funds and in allowing management to divide with the government (and thereby obscure) its responsibility for efficient operation. One should not be misled by the prestige that "systems analysis" has acquired in government circles into thinking that complex questions of resource allocation yield easily to definite answers through application of quantitative tools.[187] Judgmental, intuitive factors remain highly important. A good example of this point is the controversy, alluded to in an earlier footnote,[188] over a fifth transatlantic cable. The question that the Federal Communications Commission had to decide was whether to authorize the cable, as A.T. & T. and the other applicants urged, or to rely on satellite communications to meet the demand that the cable was designed to meet. Some of the relevant factors could be quantified, but some of the most important, such as demand in the relevant period, the completion dates of alternative facilities, what mixture of different kinds of communications facility was indicated to assure continuity of service in the event of outages, and the probable costs of facilities not yet developed, were unavoidably matters of judgment and estimation. One can perhaps criticize the Commission for failing even to attempt an estimation of the costs of the cable in the face of some attractive satellite alternatives, but it is difficult to see how the Commission could have refused the application without making the kind of judgment that, with all the system analysts in the world at its elbow, would still be well within the area

[187]For discussions of system analysis that stress the limitations as well as the strengths of the technique see C. HITCH & R. McKEAN, THE ECONOMICS OF DEFENSE IN THE NUCLEAR AGE (1960); R. McKEAN, EFFICIENCY IN GOVERNMENT THROUGH SYSTEMS ANALYSIS (1958).

[188]*See* note 138 *supra*.

of proper business discretion. To be sure, there may be cases of such egregious corporate error as to make it both proper and practical for the agency to overrule a management spending decision. But this is a doubtful basis for a substantial augmentation of the resources devoted to regulation, in the absence of any indication of how frequent and significant such errors are likely to be and whether they are beyond the existing capabilities of the agencies to perceive and correct.

In sum, we are probably stuck with the anomalous condition noted earlier: The attempt to regulate profits fosters inefficiencies unlikely to arise in the absence of regulation. Since those inefficiencies could injure society much more than monopoly profits, an indispensable adjunct to any program of profit control is effective scrutiny of the firm's expenditures. Yet the agencies have failed to exercise such scrutiny, and as we have just seen, their default is not easily cured. To state the problem most starkly, we know that profit regulation might impair the incentive of regulated firms to innovate and that innovation probably contributes more to social welfare than static efficiency does. At the same time, it is clear that we do not have and are not likely to develop the necessary analytic and institutional tools for instilling proper incentives in a regulated firm, or, failing that, for directing the firm's inventive activity by governmental decree.

D. *Changing the Procedures, Structure, or Locus of Regulatory Agencies*

Students of the regulatory process, especially those whose background is law, have been more interested in the procedures and structure of regulatory agencies, and in the agencies' relationship to the judicial, legislative, and executive branches of government, than in the substantive policies of regulation. Many interesting questions are involved in these areas,[189] but answering all of them correctly would leave unsolved the essential problems of regulation discussed in this Article. To be sure, there is no bright line between procedure and substance—between organization for policymaking and the policies themselves. For example, whether administrative proce-

---

[189]*See, e.g.*, L. JAFFE, JUDICIAL CONTROL OF ADMINISTRATIVE ACTION (1965). The major proposals for administrative reform are considered in W. CARY, POLITICS AND THE REGULATORY AGENCIES 132–39 (1967); H. FRIENDLY, *supra* note 186.

dures are more or less judicial in form may affect such vital questions as the duration of regulatory lags (presumably longer if highly judicial procedures must be followed before a company can be ordered to revise its rate schedule), the difficulty of new entry (presumably greater if highly formal proceedings are conducted on applications for certificates of public convenience and necessity), and the feasibility of making direct appraisals of efficiency (presumably somewhat greater if more flexible procedures can be devised). The political pressures that beset regulatory agencies might be somewhat alleviated by moving the regulatory agencies into executive departments, where the tradition of congressional intervention is less strong and where officials and staff are not so likely to be wholly wrapped up in a single industry (although many executive agencies, such as the Maritime Administration, which is nominally subordinate to the Secretary of Commerce, have managed to maintain substantial autonomy from executive supervision and close ties to a specific industry).

For present purposes, we need not discuss at length these and cognate possibilities (such as giving commissioners longer terms or separating policymaking from adjudication). They are essentially concerned with making the regulatory process a more effective and streamlined vehicle for implementing the conventional principles of regulation.[190] Since those principles seem to me questionable, I have difficulty viewing such administrative improvements as an unmixed blessing. In some areas, "improvement" could be disastrous—for example, if it took the form of accelerating rate proceedings to the point of preventing regulated firms from ever obtaining supracompetitive profits by virtue of regulatory lag. For what it may be worth, my own guess is that most of the proposals in this area do not promise clear-cut improvement by anyone's lights. Judicialization of regulatory proceedings may be a vice; but the conduct of regulatory business off the record, beyond public and judicial scrutiny, is manifestly an equal vice. Relocation of the regulatory agencies in the Executive Branch offers little hope, on the basis of past experience, for improvement of the regulatory process. And the separation of policymaking from adjudication reflects a rather naive conception of the

---

[190]A possible exception would be the development of adequate procedures for the expeditious determination of corporate efficiency—but I see no procedural improvement that would accomplish this.

process of policy formulation, in which adjudication has played a large and honored role.

IV. Alternatives and Recommendations

Our analysis of proposals for reforming public utility regulation confirms our preliminary conclusion that its contribution to social and economic welfare is very possibly negative. The benefits of regulation are dubious, not only because the evils of natural monopoly are exaggerated but also because the effectiveness of regulation in controlling them is highly questionable. At the same time, regulation costs a great deal and would probably cost much more if serious effort were made to prevent the undesirable side effects on efficiency that profit regulation fosters. Regulation may be likened to the treatment of an ailment whose gravity is not known with a costly and dangerous drug whose efficacy is highly uncertain. It can be improved, but I do not see how we can realistically hope to transform it into a fruitful instrument for advancing the public welfare.

To many this will seem too sweeping, too inclusive a condemnation, one that fails to compare the benefits and costs of particular regulatory controls in particular industrial settings. An institution that has pernicious effects in the case of airlines or natural-gas producers may, it will be said, have redeeming virtues in the context of the local electric utility. I consider such a particularistic approach unduly static. It is quite true that at any point in time the case for regulation is stronger in some regulated industries than in others, depending on the degree to which conditions of natural monopoly are actually present. But natural monopoly conditions are quite likely to be transient. The degree of monopoly power possessed by railroads has declined enormously in the last 40 years. The same period has seen a number of once-powerful monopolies disappear or decline, such as ice companies, street railways, and the Western Union Telegraph Company. Communications is a contemporary example of an industry undergoing rapid technological changes that are apparently opening up a host of new competitive opportunities. In general, the tempo of change in the economy seems to be increasing. The most pernicious feature of regulation would appear to be precisely its impact on change—its tendency to retard the growth of competition that would erode the power of regulated monopolists. To embrace regulation because an industry is today a natural monopoly and seems likely to remain so is to gamble dangerously with the future. To impose regulation on the basis of a prophecy that the industry will remain monopolistic forever may be to make the prophecy self-fulfilling.[191]

A. *Public Ownership*

One possible alternative to regulation is government ownership of enterprises that provide services under conditions of natural monopoly. The most attractive characteristic of the public monopoly is that it can be directed to equate price to marginal cost,[192] practicing only enough price discrimination to avert a deficit. Efficient allocation is thus ensured and monopoly profits avoided. The major difficulty is the absence of a profit incentive. Many institutions, of course, are not operated on the profit principle—government agencies and universities, for example. However, as the Soviet Union has tacitly acknowledged, no one has yet discovered an adequate substitute for profits as the driving force of industrial efficiency in an advanced economy.

The elimination of the profit incentive seems a high price to pay for efficient allocation and the elimination of monopoly profits, when at least the second objective could equally well be achieved, or at least approximated, by directing the public enterprise to maximize profits and by proportioning the managers' compensation to the profits obtained, thus preserving an element of profit incentive.[193] Under this revised model of the public monopoly, monopoly profits would accrue to the government, which could then distribute them in accordance with public need. One possible distribution would be a rebate to the customers of the enterprise.

Although this seems the preferable arrangement for a public monopoly, one would still be concerned about the elimination of the disciplinary effect of the capital market and the threat, attenuated as it may be, of a corporate take-over. One would also worry about pol-

---

[191]For a view of regulation that essentially parallels my own see M. FRIEDMAN, CAPITALISM AND FREEDOM 28–29 (1962).

[192]Subject to "second best" qualifications. *See* text accompanying note 24 *supra*.

[193]The Soviet Union and other Communist nations are experimenting with such an approach. *See, e.g.,* Harcourt, *The Measurement of the Rate of Profit and the Bonus Scheme for Managers in the Soviet Union,* 18 OXFORD ECON. PAPERS (N.S.) 58 (1966); Krylov, Rotshtein & Tsarov, *On the Procedure and Conditions for Changing to the New System,* in 2 PLANNING, PROFIT AND INCENTIVES IN THE USSR 255 (M. Sharpe ed. 1966).

itics and about change. A public enterprise would seem especially susceptible to pressure from political interest groups to depart from efficient operation in such vital areas of business management as price and wage policy, hiring policy, and plant location. Since, as was pointed out earlier, the long-run consumer interest is one of the least effectively represented in the political process, the politicization of the regulated services would appear to be highly undesirable from the standpoint of the overall welfare of our society. But perhaps the danger of political control could be minimized by creating a separate government corporation. It might be wise in addition to provide that only some members of its board of directors be appointed by the President (or state governor), and the rest by the board itself.

The least tractable problem of public monopoly, I suspect, would be change. As previously emphasized, changes in consumer tastes or in technology can alter a market from naturally monopolistic to naturally competitive. A public enterprise might thus find itself in competition with private firms. We know from history that such competition tends to be awkward and acrimonious and to yield quickly to a division of markets. It is not surprising, to take two examples, that private entities are forbidden to offer postal service and that the Tennessee Valley Authority is narrowly circumscribed in its authority to compete with private electrical companies.[194] Public and private enterprises operate under such different patterns of privilege and restraint that competitive equality would be exceedingly difficult to achieve. To be sure, insofar as public enterprises could be divorced from political influence and their operations placed on a thoroughly businesslike basis (for example, no tax exemptions), fair competition with private enterprises might become possible. Even then, one wonders what the reaction of the government would be when a nice source of revenue—the monopoly profits of one of the public enterprises—was jeopardized by private competition.

Public ownership has the further disadvantage of providing only a partial solution to the problems of public utility and common carrier regulation. It would be difficult to justify public ownership of industries such as aviation and natural-gas production that are not naturally monopolistic and where there is accordingly no convincing basis for distrusting the performance of private enterprise. Yet it is

[194]See 18 U.S.C. §§ 1696, 1729 (1964); 16 U.S.C. § 831n-4 (1964); Harden v. Kentucky Util. Co., 390 U.S. 1 (1968).

precisely in industries that are regulated despite the absence of natural monopoly that regulation is least justifiable.

Even ignoring these drawbacks, one is hard pressed to show that public ownership would be markedly superior to complete deregulation, in terms of principle or of feasibility. Neither alternative seems practical as a political matter. The one supposed advantage of public enterprise, its distributive effect, seems, for reasons explored earlier in this Article, somewhat marginal, and, as soon to be discussed, may be achievable without public ownership by means of the relatively costless solution of a modest change in the federal tax laws.

B. *Dissolution*

Another alternative to regulation, besides public ownership, is to dismember natural monopolists and to prevent their reemergence by either limiting the permissible plant scale or by forbidding mergers and limiting price competition. The drawback to this luddite solution is that it would entail the sacrifice of known and substantial economic benefits—those flowing from efficient scale—for a conjectural improvement in performance from competition. While our earlier analysis showed that competition was conducive to efficiency and innovation, it also showed that natural monopoly, so long as it is not reinforced by legal protections against entry and competition, cannot be shown to imply seriously unsatisfactory performance.

C. *Repeal of Public Utility and Common Carrier Legislation*

In principle, the repeal of public utility and common carrier legislation emerges as an attractive goal of public policy. To be sure, our reckoning of the costs and benefits of regulation contained many speculative elements. However, considering the enormous challenges that face every level of American government today, it seems reasonable to ask the supporters of a government program to bear the burden of showing that it is likely to produce a net social gain. The resources and energies of government should be directed to problems that we know are substantial, that we think are tractable to government action, and that cannot be left to the private sector to work out. There are plenty of those problems, and it is doubtful that natural monopoly is among them.

One could argue that when the question is whether to abandon rather than whether to institute a government program, the burden of proof should shift to the opponents; they must show that the direct and indirect costs of the program clearly outweigh its benefits. Under this test, perhaps public utility and common carrier regulation would be reprieved. The discussion has taken an academic turn, however, for in any event deregulation is probably not a practical objective. Even if the intellectual climate changed and fundamental criticisms of the regulatory process became more fashionable, the interests of firms for which regulation is a shield against competition, of those that fear that the abandonment of regulation would lead to expropriation by the Government, and of individuals whose employment or sense of purpose in life requires the assumption that regulation plays a vital role in the achievement of social justice and economic welfare, would constitute, along with sheer inertia and a natural reluctance to dismantle venerable institutions on grounds that are largely speculative, a decisive impediment to abandonment.

D. *Excess-Profits Tax*

A somewhat more realistic objective, perhaps, would be (1) the deregulation of those industries that are not natural monopolies, such as natural-gas production, aviation, and trucking, and, (2) in the other regulated industries, (a) removal of restrictions on entry and of controls over specific rates and (b) substitution of an excess-profits tax for regulatory limitations of overall profits. The case for the deregulation of industries that are not natural monopolies seems overwhelming. Whatever the industry structure, moreover, regulation of entry and of specific rates seems to serve little function other than to foster unnatural monopoly and gratuitously limit competition. Although the argument for retaining these controls is strengthened if overall profits remain limited,[195] it is still not convincing, especially if an excess-profits tax is substituted for the regulatory profit ceiling. A tax would minimize the disincentive and other perverse effects of profit regulation—assuming the tax rate was moderate—because it would permit the regulated firm to keep a substantial portion of any profits it could make. At the same time, the tax would require the regulated firm to divide its monopoly profits with the public.

To illustrate, suppose that in place of profit regulation a surtax of 20 percent were imposed on profits in excess of the fair rate of return

[195]*See* text accompanying notes 133–37 *supra.*

determined by the agency. The agency would still be required to compute the fair return, and to that extent the proposal does not permit us to do away with the costly processes of regulation. On the other hand, the agency would not have to concern itself with the actual rates charged by the company; in contrast to incentive regulation it would not have to monitor the firm's efficiency; and the public would have the satisfaction of knowing that 72 percent (normal corporate income tax plus surtax) of any monopoly profits would be extracted from the monopolist and used for public purposes. Such a solution, while far from ideal, would in large part answer to the popular objection to monopoly—its distributive effect—and probably with fewer undesirable side effects than under the present system of flat rate ceilings.[196]

E. *Some Practical Suggestions*

The intermediate approach just sketched has little better prospect for imminent adoption than does complete deregulation. But even without basic legislative revision, there is much that can be done in the near term to mitigate the harmful effects of regulation. A sound public policy toward regulation would have the following immediate goals: relaxation of regulatory controls as a matter of administrative discretion; upgrading of education and, with the assistance of the agencies, intensification of research in the public utility area; adoption of economically sound principles of rate design; and—especially—resolute refusal to extend regulation to new industries.

(1) Assuming that Congress and state legislatures will not remove any regulatory controls in the near future, there is still no reason why regulatory agencies cannot on their own do much to lighten the practical impact of regulation and why the President and state governors, in making appointments to the regulatory agencies, cannot appoint individuals committed to relaxing regulatory controls. This is not a

---

[196]The effectiveness of a tax on excess profits as a method of correcting the distributive effect of monopoly profits depends on the monopolist's not being able to pass it on to his customers. However, the traditional view that a profit tax is not passed on may require considerable qualification. For contrasting views on this question, *compare* M. KRYZANIAK & R. MUSGRAVE, THE SHIFTING OF THE CORPORATION INCOME TAX (1963), *with* Gordon, *The Incidence of the Corporation Income Tax in U.S. Manufacturing, 1925–62,* 57 AM. ECON. REV. 731 (1967). For a discussion of various schemes of taxing monopolists see W. BAUMOL, WELFARE ECONOMICS AND THE THEORY OF THE STATE 103–13 (2d ed. 1965). Before any such scheme were actually adopted, the vital question of its incidence would, of course, have to be considered carefully.

suggestion that the legislative purpose be defied or evaded. Regulatory mandates are characteristically cast in broad and general terms, and when one looks behind the mandate a single or simple legislative purpose is rarely to be discerned. In these circumstances regulators are entitled to conclude that a rate is not unjust or unreasonable merely because it includes monopoly profits, if the opportunity to obtain such profits is deemed to provide an indispensable incentive to efficient and progressive operation from which society will ultimately derive greater benefits than from immediately lower prices. They are entitled to conclude that the grant of a certificate of public convenience and necessity to any firm that applies for it is an appropriate policy because it will promote competition and reduce the costs of regulation.

The principal danger in administrative relaxation of regulatory controls is that it will be selective rather than across the board. Selective relaxation could have quite undesirable consequences. If, for example, the agency raised the ceiling on profits while continuing to restrict entry, its action would gratuitously enhance the ability of the firm to extract monopoly profits, because the threat of potential competition would be minimized. If the agency removed entry controls while keeping a tight lid on profits, it might prevent the incumbent firm from earning a fair return under the riskier conditions created by the elimination of the regulatory barrier to entry. A sound policy of relaxation of regulatory controls thus requires an even application.

(2) A particularly desirable change of emphasis for the regulatory agencies would be from regulation to research and analysis.[197] The agencies have broad powers to gather data on the conduct and performance of their regulatees. These powers could be used to learn more about the economic characteristics of the regulated industries and the actual effects of regulation. It is striking how little we know about the effects of regulation, or, for that matter, about the effects of monopoly. The agencies have the power to command the production of data that might shed considerable light on these questions.

Greater efforts by the agencies along these lines are unlikely to be fruitful, however, unless the members of the relevant academic disciplines—the economists, political scientists, and lawyers—give sub-

---

[197]A landmark in this respect is FEDERAL POWER COMMISSION, NATIONAL POWER SURVEY (1964).

stantially more effective consideration to the problems of regulation. We need empirical studies of how regulatory agencies actually operate; what costs regulation imposes on regulated firms; what its impact is on rates and profits; and what measures regulated firms take to "get around" regulation, how effective such measures are, and what social costs they impose. We also need much more careful exploration of possible improvements in and alternatives to the conventional regulatory controls. One is taxation. Another promising possibility is the development of the procedures and institutions necessary for effective bargaining between customers and prospective monopolists as a substitute for regulation—a point to which we shall return briefly in a moment. Much of this research, to be effective, will have to be interdisciplinary. An increased emphasis on empirical, interdisciplinary research at the university level, together with more effective fact-gathering by the agencies themselves, might soon produce answers to many of the crucial questions that I have been forced to discuss in conjectural terms—and that if answered could substantiate or disprove the highly negative reflections that are the heart of this Article.

(3) An early dividend of an improved research effort might be the adoption of sounder pricing principles. Utility rate structures, as we have seen, are apparently rather inefficient, at least partly as a result of regulatory adherence to outmoded and ill-considered fairness notions that require internal subsidization and prevent discrimination regardless of competitive and efficiency considerations. Much of the regulatory support of inefficient pricing is based not upon a deliberate subordination of efficiency to other social goals, but rather, I am convinced, on failure to understand what is inefficient and socially harmful about the existing rate structures. This failure should be remediable if the academic profession bends its educative talents to the task. One distinction that particularly requires to be hammered home by economists is between price discrimination by an unregulated monopolist and discrimination by a monopolist whose profits are effectively constrained. In the former case, it cannot be proved rigorously that output would be larger than if a single price were charged; in the latter case, it is very likely that output will be larger. Discrimination (so long as it involves no sales below marginal cost) will enable the company's fixed costs to be spread over a larger output, thereby enabling rates to be reduced. Of course, to the extent that profits are not effectively limited by regulation, we cannot be

sure that discrimination will make the existing customers better off. Assuming, however, that profit regulation has some effect, it seems good policy to encourage the natural monopolist to discriminate.

(4) One hears talk of extending public utility regulation to new industries, such as data processing[198] or, more plausibly, the community-antenna television industry.[199] If CATV should develop to the point where no over-the-air service is available in some communities or, more probably, where the programming choices available on the cable are so much greater as to make over-the-air service an inadequate substitute, we would be in the presence of a new natural monopoly; for duplicate wire grids would be as wasteful in this context as in that of electrical or telephone service to the home. I would argue strongly that this circumstance should not justify the imposition of regulation, because we have no basis for believing that the net social gain of regulating natural monopoly is positive. Here, incidentally, is an instance where the bargaining process might be an effective substitute for regulation. A local community, as a condition to permitting a particular CATV operator the use of public rights-of-way, could bargain with it over the level of rates that the operator would charge subscribers in the community.[200] The community should be in a strong bargaining position, for there are normally several CATV operators interested in wiring any given community. I am not prepared to press this suggestion too far, since history appears to contain a large number of examples where such bargains turned out to be quite bad from the public's point of view.[201] Moreover, there may be a great temptation to offer the CATV operator an exclusive franchise in exchange for an agreement not to increase its rates—an arrangement that may be tantamount to regulation. But that is an aside. The essential point is that the logical and empirical founda-

---

[198]See Irwin, *The Computer Utility: Competition or Regulation?*, 76 YALE L.J. 1299 (1967).

[199]See Barnett & Greenberg, *A Proposal for Wired City Television*, 1968 WASH. U.L.Q. I.

[200]This is not a suggestion that the operator's prospective monopoly profits be capitalized in a franchise fee paid the city, which would succeed in capturing the monopoly profits for the public but at whatever cost in allocative inefficiency monopoly pricing of the service might impose. Rather, the city on behalf of its residents should negotiate with each applicant the rates at which he will agree to provide service to the residents. If this should prove infeasible, however, exaction of a lump-sum franchise fee, or perhaps of annual fees, might be considered as a way of ameliorating at least the distributional effects of the monopoly.

[201]See, e.g., M. GLAESER, PUBLIC UTILITIES IN AMERICAN CAPITALISM 32–39 (1957).

tions of common carrier and public utility regulation are too shaky to support further extensions.

I attach particular importance to this last recommendation. In the first place, unlike some others, it seems eminently attainable. When the issue is whether to extend rather than whether to withdraw regulation, the weight of inertia is against regulation. There has been no major extension of regulation since the 1930's, when the nation, traumatized by the Great Depression, reached the nadir of its faith in private enterprise.[202] In the second place, among the realistic policy options in this area, nonextension offers the most substantial prospect for the eventual elimination of regulation—the direction in which, on the basis of present evidence, I believe we should move. In the long run, there may be few natural monopolies, perhaps none, such is the pace of change in consumer taste and in technology in a dynamic economy. It is not completely fanciful to envisage a time in which electric utilities will have to compete with manufacturers of nuclear-powered home generators or telephone companies with CATV operators. If regulation is not extended to embrace potential competitors of regulated firms, it may eventually wither away.

[202]To be sure, in 1954 the Supreme Court in Phillips Petroleum Co. v. Wisconsin, 347 U.S. 672 (1954), extended the FPC's regulatory authority to natural-gas producers. But the Court was interpreting the Natural Gas Act, 15 U.S.C. §§ 717–717w (1964), passed in 1938.

About the Author

Richard A. Posner graduated from Yale College in 1959, *summa cum laude.* He graduated first in his class from Harvard Law School in 1962, *magna cum laude,* and was President of the *Harvard Law Review.* He worked for several years in Washington during the Kennedy and Johnson Administrations—as law clerk to Justice William J. Brennan, Jr., as an assistant to Commissioner Philip Elman of the Federal Trade Commission, as an assistant to the Solicitor General of the U.S., Thurgood Marshall, and as general counsel of President Johnson's Task Force on Communications Policy.

Posner entered law teaching in 1968 at Stanford as an associate professor, and became professor of law at the University of Chicago Law School in 1969, where he remained (later as Lee and Brena Freeman Professor of Law) until his appointment to the Seventh Circuit in 1981. During this period Posner wrote a number of books (including *Antitrust Law: An Economic Perspective, Economic Analysis of Law*—now in its fourth edition—and *The Economics of Justice).* He founded the *Journal of Legal Studies,* primarily to encourage economic analysis of law, and has been appointed along with Orley Ashenfelter as the first editor of the *American Law and Economics Review,* the journal of the American Law and Economic Association.

Posner is Chief Judge of the U.S. Court of Appeals for the Seventh Circuit. He continues to teach part time at the University of Chicago Law School, where he is Senior Lecturer, and to write academic articles and books. He has written 25 books and more than 250 articles and book reviews. His academic work since his becoming a judge has included studies in the economics of criminal law, labor law, and intellectual property; in jurisprudence, law and literature, and the interpretation of constitutional and statutory texts; and in the economics of sexuality and of old age. His recent books include *Private Choices and Public Health: The AIDS Epidemic in an Economic Perspective* (1993) (coauthored with Tomas Philipson), *Overcoming Law* (1995), *Aging and Old Age* (1995), a second edition of *The Federal Courts* (1996), *Law and Legal Theory in England and America* (1996), a fifth edition of *Economic Analysis of Law* (1997), and a revised and enlarged edition of *Law and Literature* (1998). His latest book, *The Problematics of Moral and Legal Theory,* will appear in 1999.

Cato Institute

Founded in 1977, the Cato Institute is a public policy research foundation dedicated to broadening the parameters of policy debate to allow consideration of more options that are consistent with the traditional American principles of limited government, individual liberty, and peace. To that end, the Institute strives to achieve greater involvement of the intelligent, concerned lay public in questions of policy and the proper role of government.

The Institute is named for *Cato's Letters*, libertarian pamphlets that were widely read in the American Colonies in the early 18th century and played a major role in laying the philosophical foundation for the American Revolution.

Despite the achievement of the nation's Founders, today virtually no aspect of life is free from government encroachment. A pervasive intolerance for individual rights is shown by government's arbitrary intrusions into private economic transactions and its disregard for civil liberties.

To counter that trend, the Cato Institute undertakes an extensive publications program that addresses the complete spectrum of policy issues. Books, monographs, and shorter studies are commissioned to examine the federal budget, Social Security, regulation, military spending, international trade, and myriad other issues. Major policy conferences are held throughout the year, from which papers are published thrice yearly in the *Cato Journal*. The Institute also publishes the quarterly magazine *Regulation*.

In order to maintain its independence, the Cato Institute accepts no government funding. Contributions are received from foundations, corporations, and individuals, and other revenue is generated from the sale of publications. The Institute is a nonprofit, tax-exempt, educational foundation under Section 501(c)3 of the Internal Revenue Code.

CATO INSTITUTE
1000 Massachusetts Ave., N.W.
Washington, D.C. 20001